What I'm Going to Be When They Grow Up

BY DOROTHY PEREZ

with Jenna Quentin
Cover art by Adrian Buentello

Thank you for all the love & support!

Library of Congress Control Number: 2014921330
CreateSpace Independent Publishing Platform
North Charleston, South Carolina

DEDICATION

I am dedicating this book to the memory of Manuel because without his help, love and wisdom this life would not have been possible. I'm grateful to him for helping me to have my large family and that we were in this together. I also want to thank our older children because I know there were many times that extra hours were spent on our extended family since our foster children often came with problems beyond their control.

What a wonderful life.

Dorothy

Index

Preface

THIS BOOK IS A COMBINATION of interviews with Dorothy, stories she wrote for her Memory Makers group, articles, and Manuel's notes and letters found in a binder a few days after he passed away. He had been writing these notes for a long time without his family's knowledge. What a treasure!

The cover art is based off a birthday card from Dorothy's dear friend and Parson's art teacher, Arlita McClure. A talented artist, Adrian Buentello from Newton, Kansas, remastered and designed this art around Arlista's. The flags represent Manuel's Mexican heritage, with Dorothy's Swedish and German background, as they raised their multi-colored family in the USA. Like the old woman who lived in the shoe, Dorothy had many children—however, I think she knew just what to do!

These stories are from Dorothy or Manuel's viewpoint, and reflect only how they saw or remembered things. We have tried to neither withhold the hard nor the triumphant parts of these stories. We have changed the names of foster children and others for their privacy. Perhaps someday, the next version of this book featuring interviews with the foster children, now adults looking back at their childhood.

CHAPTER ONE

How We Started Fostering

IN DOROTHY'S WORDS :
I always wanted a large family. My dream was twelve children, and my husband Manuel wasn't opposed to the idea. Well, my goal was more than met. We raised ninety-four children in our home in Parsons, Kansas, and that doesn't count the many overnighters.

Instead of a mother's ring with a few birthstones, I have a mother's necklace with dozens of miniature pictures and charms with birth dates that reminds me of Bliss, Bobby, Roland, Christine, and so many others. But not even this keepsake contains all their names.

As I look back, I've always wondered how we did it. I always say I have a big heart but not much brain. I've always loved being Dorothy from Kansas, like in the Wizard of Oz, but maybe I am bit of a Scarecrow. If I had a brain, would I have begun foster care? Definitely, yes.

MY GRANDPARENTS ON THEIR WEDDING DAY.

Fostering started in my family more than one hundred years ago with my grandparents, Emil and Mary Linderholm. The day after they were married, they became the parents of a baby girl. A close friend died in childbirth. The father was frantic because he had two other children. He asked my grandparents to take the baby until he could get life all figured out.

The baby became my Aunt Annette, who never left our family – she was the oldest of seven girls. My mother, the youngest, was two-years-old when her father died at the young age of forty in 1912. Her mother had to take care of raising the girls.

Another branch of the family, my great aunt and uncle, enlarged their family with a boy off the infamous "Kansas

Orphan Train." During this movement, 150,000-200,000 children were brought ot the MidWest from the streets of Eastern cities from 1860s to 1930s.

1960s

My fostering began in September 1963 when I got a call from Social and Rehabilitation Services (now the Department for Children and Families). I thought it was because I'd contacted them about adoption. We had four boys of our own at that point.

To my shock, social services had seven siblings who needed a home for the night. They selected us because Manuel was a special education teacher and all these children had special needs and mental handicaps. We had no idea of being foster parents at that time.

We were overwhelmed at the thought of eleven kids in our house but said yes. Well, our lives changed forever.

There were five girls and two boys, ages six to sixteen-years-old. Their mother had recently died at the age of thirty-eight, possibly from malnutrition while pregnant. All together, there were ten children. The youngest two were left in the custody of their father, the mother's current boyfriend. The oldest was already eighteen-years-old and on his own.

They were friendly, loving kids. I had figured that I would have seven kids bawling over the death of their mother. However, they had picked flowers for me. Many of the children who came to us later were angry with their situation and the world. The Nelsons were sweet kids, not belligerent at all.

Social services wanted all seven children to go to the Parsons State Hospital for retarded children, however it couldn't accomodate all of them so quickly. Their overnight stay with us turned into days, which turned into weeks, until it was clear they would stay long term.

We didn't have a foster license, but the state worked it so that we could accommodate the Nelsons. There were other times later that they changed our license to allow us to have more children.

Of course, our house wasn't big enough at the time. The authorities wanted to place some of them at the State Hospital, but my mom agreed to take the three older children, two girls and a boy. My father had recently passed away and Mom said she'd do what she could.

They didn't make it easy on Mom. Emma didn't want to go to school at the State Hospital, so once she locked the truck and hid the key. Jimmy, didn't like bathing, so before his workday began, Manuel would go over to Mom's to bathe him.

The Nelsons arrived in September, however we didn't receive state funding until March, for whatever reason. That was just when Manuel had started teaching in the Parons public high school. He was employed by the Tri-County Special Education Co-Op with a lower salary than when he worked at the Parsons State Hospital.

These children had fallen into our laps to feed and clothe, so our budget was understandably skimpy at the time. Our little Martin remembered going to the Dairy Queen. As we passed it one day, he said, "Mama, I been askin' you and askin' you for an ice cream cone and you never buy me one any more!" It was hard to explain to the baby of our family, why there were suddenly so many others to share with. Our children have grown up to be caring people, so I don't think they suffered too much.

The Nelson children were survivors. Manuel believed survival took precedence over learning and being underfed could have contributed to their learning disabilities. We found that none of them could read well.

It was three weeks before I could convince them that they'd get enough food. With four boys, we were used to busy, noisy

4

meals—now that was amplified. The Nelson children ate quickly, desperate to get more before it was all gone.

I had to adjust how much food to make. An insurance man stopped by one evening and saw the piles of fried chicken on the table.

"Dorothy, are you going on a picnic?"

I laughed and said, "No, my life has become a picnic!"

I would find food stockpiled in the children's beds, parts of apples or popcorn. They wanted to be sure they'd have something to eat later.

The youngest girl was a blonde eight-year-old named Joan. She threw up all the time. The doctor thought it was because she wasn't used to proper food. Beans and pancakes seemed to be foods she could keep down for a while. Those children could eat a ton of beans!

Bobby was the youngest. When he was nine-years-old or so, he helped with the paper route our four boys had always done. It was at this point that we noticed Bobby had a habit of stealing. Manuel theorized that this too stemmed from their survival skills.

Bobby would ask folks on his route if he could use their bathroom—then he'd steal something inconsequential, things a little boy couldn't want, like lipstick. By the time he was a teenager, he was stealing cars. He would just joy ride around after school. It got so bad that when a car was stolen, the police would come to our house first to question Bobby. At one time, he took the chief of police's private car.

He was with us until his eighteenth birthday, when he was arrested for stealing a car. He was caught that time because as he was stealing the car out of its owner's driveway, he ran over a pedestrain and broke her arm. This time, Bobby didn't escape. He has spent most of his life since then in and out of jail. He always says he's gonna be good, he's gonna be good.

We hadn't heard from him in a while. Then one Thanksgiving Day, he came driving up in a car with four young people and a three-month-old baby.

First thing Manuel did was to check the license plate and call the police to see if it had been stolen. He found out it belonged to a lawyer in Texas who had lent it to his daughter, the mother of the baby.

Bobby had brought his friends with the promise that his dad would let them live in one of his rental houses. Manuel was not willing to accommodate Bobby and his entourage. They stayed with us for a week and then Manuel said he was willing to pay for them to stay in a motel for a week.

Bobby showed his friends around town, where he went to school and such. While they stayed with us, they would leave the baby parked in front of the TV for hours. "It's ok; he likes TV," said Bobby. From what I understood, Bobby wasn't the child's father.

During their stay, they made trouble at the motel, and the police were called. I'm not sure on the details, but it seems the girl's dad sent money for them to go back to Texas. And they all left.

Naturally it hurt to see the child we were raising keep getting into trouble. We just kept being his parents until the police had to intervene.

When we began fostering, I don't think anyone knew what to do with foster children other than to give them a place to call home. A lot of people would have just given up on Bobby, but I don't know. I guess we're just tough.

The oldest Nelson girl, Betty, was one of the children staying with my mom. She wasn't in school at that point. She had severe special needs, including a speech impediment. She was sixteen-years-old, so she was allowed to go the store and such alone. At some point, she was raped. It was a real shock to my poor mother when it became evident that Betty was pregnant.

Mom helped Betty through the pregnancy, but the courts took her baby away from her at birth. Mom said Betty would just sit on the floor and moan for her child.

Betty went through training at the State Hospital and when she was maybe eighteen or twenty-years-old, they sent her to Newton to work at a nursing home. She would come out to visit us, taking a taxi from Newton to Wichita then a bus to Parsons, and she'd walk several miles from the station. She walked everywhere.

I got a call in the middle of the night from a sheriff in a southern state. "We found a lady walking along the highway. We don't understand her, but she has your phone number."

I immediately thought of Betty and her hard-to-understand speech. Sure enough, it was Betty. I asked her where she was and what she was doing.

She had gone to Florida with some guy and was walking back to Kansas. "I didn't like him; I'm coming back," Betty said.

I explained it all to the sheriff. He and his staff gathered enough money to send Betty on a bus back to Kansas.

In Newton, Betty got married. Once, she called me asking for $25,000 to bail her husband out of jail. "I want him out," she said. "I'm lonesome." Of course, I couldn't do that.

Some of the other children, we haven't heard from in a while, though recently I did get a call from a payday loan palce where Bobby had listed me as a reference. The youngest girl, Joan, tries to stay in touch with her siblings. She stayed with us until her marriage at age twenty-two. Her husband was the son of some dear old friends of ours, Tom and Beth, from Minnesota.

Beth's mother still lived in Parsons, and they come to visit her, or we'd take our camper up to them. One trip their son, Kevin, who also had special needs and disabilities, took a fancy to our Joan.

His father was ill, and one of his dying requests was to see Manuel again. We hurried up to Minnesota, just a week before

Tom passed. Six weeks later, Beth and Kevin came to Parsons to visit her mother. One evening, Beth and I were walking and talking. The subject of our two love-struck children came up, along with Kevin and Joan's special needs. Joan went back with them to Minnesota to marry Kevin. Joan named her first son after Manuel.

Minnesota's cold bothered Kevin's lung condition, however. He, Joan and their two children moved back to Parsons and lived in one of our rental houses. Joan was always a hard worker—she worked at Sonic in high school, and then in nursing homes. Kevin never worked and drew a disability check. Eventually, Joan and Kevin divorced. Joan still lives close by and calls me every couple days.

SOON AFTER THE NELSONS ARRIVED 1963.

Over the years of fostering, I've collected different thoughts and philosophies. Foster mother and author Anna Perrot Rose wrote the way I think. I have often used her 1950 book, "Room for One More," as it fits well with our lifestyle. Rose says, "Long ago, I formed a theory about foster parents. In spite of wide, varied and often conflicting views on raising children, they have one trait in common: they are the kind of parents who expect children to behave. That is why they can take in extra children, usually ones with special problems and desperate needs.

"It isn't that we came equipped with special insulation against the disagreeable things connected with kids like, noise, dirt, destruction, disobedience. That isn't exactly true, but they are largely the sort of people who can say calmly, 'Cut it out... that's enough' and cheerfully make it stick."

CHAPTER TWO

Our Baby Bliss

Late 1920s-1930s

IN DOROTHY'S WORDS:

My parents, Milbert and Georgia Meier, met at an ice skating party for maids and butlers in Kansas City. My mother had gotten the job as a maid after high school, and my father had moved from a farm to the city and worked as a butler.

I was born in Kansas City, Kansas in 1928 at the beginning of the Great Depression. Though my parents were Lutherans, I was born in a Catholic hospital. My mother named me after the nurse, Sister Dorothy. I've enjoyed also sharing this name with the Kansas girl in the Wizard of Oz.

My father delivered bread in a horse-drawn wagon for Manor Bakery and we lived in a nice brick house. When he lost his job, my

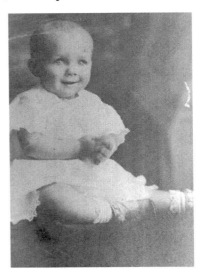

DOROTHY AS A BABY.

10

parents lost our home to the bank, like many other families in those hard times.

I was two or three-years old, and my brother John was a baby when we moved to Lindsborg, Kansas, to live with my maternal grandma. Eventually, we got a little house across the alley from Grandma. I was five-years-old when my brother Leonard was born.

In 1934, when I was six-years-old, my dad found work in Liberty, Missouri. My mother took me on a tour of the school I would attend. When the principal showed us the kindergarten room, I was amazed to see the children taking naps on the floor. I was going to school to learn, not take a nap.

I don't remember the first time I saw the movie, "The Wizard of Oz," but I was eleven-years-old when it came to theaters and I have always loved being associated with Dorothy. My parents would let us go to the Saturday morning matinée, because it only cost a dime those days.

1940s

When I was a about fifteen-years-old in Liberty, a Kansas City agency called my mother in desperation. I don't know how they knew her. There was a Catholic orphanage with so many babies that they were never taken out of their cribs unless they were being fed or bathed.

My mother agreed to take in nine-month-old George. I don't know if she wanted more children, but she had lost two babies and her older sisters in Lindsborg had large families. Mom became the first foster mother in Clay County, Missouri.

George couldn't crawl or move around much because he had rarely been out of bed. He didn't even talk for his age. He was a funny little baby, with blonde curls—I thought he looked like

11

Harpo Marx. He had some kind of a condition that made his whole arm turn red and purple when it got cold.

Then in 1945, my parents bought a farm in Parsons. George was not allowed to cross state lines to accompany us. Leaving him was hard—I'd helped care for him and loved him in the year and a half or so that we had him.

This was my first experience with my least favorite thing about fostering—building attachments and then the children leave, for one reason or another.

This story repeated itself in my life years later with Bliss. Much like George, we couldn't keep her with us.

Late 1970s-1980s

Bliss was only six-months-old when she came to us, our first foster baby. Strangers had a hard time figuring out how we—a Mexican father and a Swedish mother—could have a curly-haired little black baby.

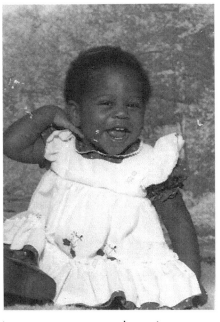

Our adopted daughters, Melissa and Rita, grew up holding her and caring for her. Our boys would finish their paper routes and then ride her around on their bikes in their newspaper bags. She was an active, passionate child.

Her grandmother, Clementine, was a teacher in town. She had felt her daughter wasn't able to care for Bliss and alerted the authorities. The courts removed Bliss from the home.

Clementine was involved in Bliss's life while she was with us. I had to take Bliss to the hospital for asthma treatments and Clementine went with me one time.

"It usually goes better if the mother holds the child," said the nurse.

"Oh, I'm not the mother," said dark-skinned Clementine. "I'm just the grandma." She pointed to Swedish blonde me. "She's the mother."

We all had a good laugh as the nurse tried to figure that out.

Clementine would come over and help me tame Bliss's frizzy curls. I didn't have much experience!

We had a foster boy, Larry, who was as blond as Bliss was dark. They were just the same sized and loved each other as small children.

We tried to adopt Bliss. She was ours, after all, our baby.

But the flawed system wouldn't let us. Because of race. We didn't match our child, and they decided Bliss would do better being raised by an African American family, than our Neapolitan family. This was in the early 1980s. I was always sad that Clementine didn't raise Bliss herself. I could have dealt with the separation better if it hadn't been out of the family.

Bliss was six-years-old when she was adopted by an African-American couple.

When they took her away, Bliss wrapped herself around the dining room table legs. She didn't understand. How could she be taken away from her family? I can still hear her screaming.

That girl was the reason I started working at Wal-Mart because I was crying all the time. I wasn't really looking for a job. I figured if I was doing something else, I'd stop crying. I walked into the store and asked if they had any openings. When I got back home, the manager called to say I was hired. I had worked at the bank before, so being a cashier wasn't too much of a change. I worked part-time, and we arranged it with Manuel's teaching schedule, so he was at home while I worked. Occasionally, we'd get a babysitter.

But I didn't forget about my baby, Bliss. I grieved like she was dead, but we knew she was alive.

Her adoptive parents lived in Olathe and said they wouldn't "erase away the years" that we'd had with her. They brought her to see us one time. She was all dolled up, so cute in a little dress with her black fuzzy hair done better than I had ever managed.

"I have to dress like this all the time," she told Rita, with a pout.

After a while, it became clear that Bliss's adoptive parents didn't want contact—they found it was too difficult. I would still try to call her on her birthday. The last time was her eighteenth birthday. I called at 9 p.m.

"No, you can't talk to her. Bliss is already asleep," said her adopted parents.

I couldn't imagine any teenage girl being in bed that early, especially not for such an important birthday. But what could I do? After that, we lost track of her.

I'm sure they must have been good people, as they were willing to adopt and all. But they were older and had adopted a boy who was already in college when they took six-year-old Bliss. I'm not sure they were ready to handle a busy little person.

2010s

Five or six years ago, Bliss found my name and address in her adoption papers and called me. She was living in Florida with her little girl. We didn't even know her adoptive parents had moved there.

"I never knew why you gave me away," said my baby girl over the phone. "I figured you didn't love me."

Such heartbreak. I asked my adopted daughters, Melissa and Rita, to call Bliss with me the next day. Of course, my girls had only been a few months old when they were adopted, and hadn't left families that they remembered.

We all talked and cried. We explained that the rules at that time wouldn't let us adopt her, even though a few years later we were able to adopt Ronald, who is also African American.

We made plans and in 2012, we went as a family group to Florida and got to see Bliss again. It was exciting. Our son Ron and his wife Sonia, Melissa and her husband Gary, and some grandkids flew out there. We filled up our van and drove out ith Martin and his family.

Unfortunately, Bliss said the adoption hadn't been a good fit. Her adopted parents refused to even acknowledge her child as their grandchild, and do not allow her to call them "Grandma and Grandpa." Her older adopted brother doesn't even speak to his parents anymore.

"I wasn't asleep on my eighteenth birthday," Bliss told me. "I knew it was you on the phone, but they wouldn't let me talk to you."

"My house is still big if you wanna come back," I told her.

CHAPTER THREE

Surviving Together

1910
IN MANUEL'S WORDS:

My father, Jose, and his brother decided to emmigrate to the USA around 1910. They had heard they could have a better life there. My mother had a total of sixteen births; eleven of those babies didn't survive to adulthood due to bad medical conditions.

The brothers left behind their loved ones to get something started in the new country before sending for their families. Perhaps due to the difficulty of crossing the border, the brothers became separated. Language, distance and means of communication were barriers as they tried to carve out a new life. Without modern conveniences for communication, it was as if their other relatives in Mexico ceased to exist.

My dad hitched a ride on the Missouri-Kansas-Texas railroad straight to Parsons, where he settled, perhaps because it was a busy railroad town at the time. He then worked for the Katy railroad for thirty-seven years. Dad decided to use the surname Perez, instead of Ramirez—we never understood why.

In 1916, he sent for his wife and my three older siblings, Joe, Frances and Mike. Then my twin sister and I were born in Parsons, Kansas, on May 18, 1923. I also had a younger sister, Delores, who we called Lola.

MANUEL AND HIS TWIN SISTER, VIRGINIA

As my parents and other Mexicans met each other in a new land, it was paramount that they group together. The spiritual bond of Catholicism created the cohesiveness that was to provide the faith and hope of a better life. I grew up in the large Mexican community of Parsons, with my three older siblings, my twin and a younger sister. When we were three-years-old, my twin sister became ill and died

1950s

For forty-five years Dad didn't know where his brother had ended up. Upon his retirement, Dad had a longing for yesteryear and he went back to their old village in Mexico. He heard rumors that a Ramirez brother had settled in Trinidad, Colorado. So Dad went to find him.

Oddly enough, the two old men were only truly sure they had found each when they recognized the names of their oldest, Mexico-born children. The brothers had indeed, found each other. Five cars of relatives drove from Colorado to Parsons to meet their long-lost cousins not long after Dorothy and I were married.

1990s Letter to Dorothy, sons and daughters: Daniel, Ron, Brian, Martin, Melissa and Rita

Song: "If You Don't Know Me By Now" you'll never, never, never know my ambitions.

I've made an attempt to give you a bird's eye view of yesteryear. Adults and peers that helped shape an aptitude, attitude and philosophy of what I am today. I grew up with some great, practical adults and peers, an understanding dad, mom and family.

My longing desire was and still is to exhibit the same love and understanding that came my way. To bring you a smile, with the nostalgic memory of days past.

Never should you feel alone, for His Grace envelopes and comforts you. Be steadfast and be a faithful steward to His Creation.

I love you. This is "our way"—loving you just as we always have.

There were so many things I still wanted to do. So many things to say to each of you whom I love. I did not fear, for in Him my faith was placed. His comforting presence gave me serenity to accept, courage to change, and the wisdom to be comforted in your presence.

Lovingly, Dad

1930s
IN MANUEL'S WORDS:
My earliest memories were as a six-year-old in 1929. Our home at 1301 Lincoln was a two-story house on the corner of Oak and Lincoln in Parsons. I shared a second-floor bedroom with my brothers, Joe and Mike.

Across the street to the west was Coys Café. More directly south was a flag house. Here, a flagman would stop traffic as trains were crossing Crawford Street. The café was a waiting place for railroad crews preparing to get aboard the train. Across the way to the south was the Katy train station.

Dad worked on the railroad as a section hand. I recall in the winter it was Dad's job to clear the snow from the train station as well as at the Crawford crossing. I remember as a child, running to meet Dad on his arrival home from work. The banana or cookie he left was looked forward to eagerly.

Dad was acquainted with a man who hauled old railroad ties. We used them to heat our home. My oldest brother, Joe, supervised us boys as we cut the ties into pieces the right size for the stove. I remember the hand saw we used. Later, we used a car's rear wheel to power a table saw for cutting the ties.

I recall my older sister Frances with her reprimands when she felt I was disrespectful to Mother. Guess she knew Mom was always giving in to me. Of course, Frances was one of the providers to the family budget, as well as Joe.

Mom was an avid gardener. There was a grape vine, a corn patch, a potato patch and general garden produce. A stream passed close to our back yard, and this was our source for watering the garden. Our backyard had oak trees, and we gathered the acorns for food. I think of the time spent helping Mom—it was together that we survived.

In spite of hard times, my parents opened their home for the Catholic Christmas Posadas (a reenactment of Mary and

Joseph's journey to Bethlehem). They also welcomed families passing through town in search of a dream, hobos working for a meal or just resting while waiting for the departure of the train.

As a nine year-old, I found an unlikely playground two or three blocks from our house—the stockyards. I made friends with the adults and became an errand boy for the truck driver for the feed store. Cleaning the store was another source of income.

I milked cows and was paid in hay and milk. Mother made cheese and butter at home. Later, I learned to choose cows for their quantity of milk.

The Labotte Creek and the ice plant were special childhood places too. Across the tracks from the feed store, sat the ice plant—my acquaintance with Mr. Burris was my ticket to free ice and ripe fruit.

One childhood memory was in 1934. After the infamous Bonnie and Clyde had been captured and killed, their bullet-riddled Ford was brought on display through town. I got to see their actual car at the Coca Cola plant.

Dad's railroad pass was Mom's ticket to travel. Somehow I don't recall missing school to go with her as we went to San Antonio, Texas, and Kansas City, Missouri.

The Union Station at Kansas City was fascinating to me—the space, people entering trains, the newspaper vendors. Kansas City became a special place as Mom came to know the family of the priest, Father Muñoz, who came later to Parsons to serve the Mexican community. He was the nucleus that brought the community together.

I don't remember the San Antonio station. The marketplace, however, was awesome—the atmosphere was very quaint and Spanish.

1970s
IN DOROTHY'S WORDS:
Some of the children we fostered were from good homes with unusual circumstances. We remember Braxton as ornery. There was a difficult situation with his dad and step-mom, who didn't

get on with him. The grandma had taken him in—I think she felt he was her responsibility. However, she was unable to continue to care for him, and he went into the system.

He came to us as a teenager in high school—I think he stayed with us for about a year. He shared a room with Jacob, who was from a Jehovah's Witness family.

Jacob was smart and good looking and came with nice clothes. Most of our kids needed new clothes when they arrived.

I understood that Jacob had left his family because he didn't want to be restrained by their religious beliefs and wanted to be like other boys—celebrating birthdays and playing basketball and such. He wasn't a bad boy.

Jacob and Braxton got into escapades together. I remember one night they climbed out the window onto the roof and down to the ground. Typical teen boy stuff.

> Dear Dorothy,
> Ever since I've been here you've never done one thing to hurt me or my feelings. I feel like I've taken advantage of you and your house. For this you don't know how much hurt and anger I feel right now. I think this home is the best place a boy could be to straighten out the problems (that is if you want to, or you just try to ignore the problem and it just gets bigger). What I'm trying to say is that if I had a mother I wish you'd be it. You're the closest thing to a real mom I ever had, or probably will ever have. I'm just sorry I had to leave this way.
> Love, Braxton

Braxton was returned to his home. Years later, while I was working at Wal-Mart, I would chat with a young man who refilled the Coke machine close to my register. He always called me

Dorothy, and if I wasn't busy, we'd have a nice talk. One day he said, "Dorothy, I don't think you know who I am. I lived with you—I'm Braxton."

He did look different all grown up. I was glad to see how he grew up.

CHAPTER FOUR

Dodging Bullets

1930s

IN MANUEL'S WORDS:

An Easter Sunday accident around 1935 changed the course of my life. I was about twelve-years-old. My big brother Joe enjoyed having friends over and they gathered at our place. I had eaten dinner and was outside playing marbles with friends. My friend Carl and I ventured into the garage to look over my older brother Joe's gun collection.

A .32 caliber pistol accidentally went off in Carl's hands, the bullet striking me in the abdomen. I passed out. Joe realized I needed immediate attention and called an ambulance. I came to in the ambulance and told the attendant, "Here it is." I could hold the bullet in my fingertips as it almost protruded from the opposite side it had entered.

I was in the hospital for six months. Dad never failed to come visit me on the weekends while I was laid up at Mercy. Mom never gave up on me. I wonder how it went at home, as I don't know if she ever left my side.

My doctor was Dr. Brady. As I began to improve, he asked what I wanted for dinner. Of course, my response was "steak and ice cream." However, the tray never failed to arrive with my special diet of crackers and chicken soup.

My nurse, Livera McCoy or Mac, was very dear to me as she was consistent in caring for me. Her conversation and respect for Mother impressed me much. In my adult years, it was good to be in touch with her, until she passed away.

I carried a very ugly incision from the gunshot incident. For a very long time, it was quite obvious where the bullet entered just above my right hip. For years, I had attacks of abdominal pain, writhing on the floor. As an adult, a doctor suggested scar tissue was inhibiting my gallbladder—once the organ was removed, the attacks stopped.

I missed a year of school when I was shot. I had attended St. Patrick's school, grade one through six. It was there that I learned English. However, my elementary years were the pits. I wish I could recall some inspirational moment of my years there. I was made a janitor at the church while school was in session, shining candlesticks rather than learning. And I wasn't the only one in this position—there were others that kept me company.

I had various tasks given me by the nuns in the school administration. Sister Anatole wanted fertilizer for her potted plants and told me to bring our chicken manure. I brought all other kinds of dirt to fool her.

Personally, I resented the sisters for using me this way. Sister Anatole threatened she would only pass me to seventh grade if I promised I would stay another year. This was at near the end of the school year.

People labeled me "Mexican-Hispanic" as if it was an insult. I set out to prove myself. Slurs that could have hurt were rather stings that awakened me. They didn't expect me to do well.

Dad and Mom, however, encouraged me to get an education. More importantly, let's say they gave me faith and confidence. It was my parents' heritage to stand erect, proud and unafraid, to think and act for myself. I didn't tell my parents, but due to my unhappiness, I decided to change schools.

I elected to go to East High in 1939 at age fifteen. I was tired of not getting my due share of learning with my peers.

I had to summon my courage to make an appointment with Principal Harry Rule at East High School. I asked him for permission to attend. Principal Rule assured me that I was welcome, even without the certified grade graduation diploma from St. Patrick's. I didn't know that there was no question of <u>not</u> being admitted, as it was a public school.

At my new high school, I found the joy of learning. Those teachers and students encouraged me to continue my education and I made many new, good friends. There was only one guy from my neighborhood who attended East High.

MANUEL STUDYING

My academic peers caused me to motivate myself. Friendly adults and teachers gave me the courage to challenge the status quo, therefore, I set high goals to achieve.

Throughout my life, I sought opportunity and took calculated risks to build a dream—to fail where I failed and achieve wherever I could. My dream? Self-sufficiency.

I was not guaranteed success, yet the thrill of fulfillment was cause to reach higher. With God's help, I've endured and have enjoyed His creation. His talents bestowed on me have given me fulfillment. Hopefully, I have been a wise steward of His gift.

1970s
IN DOROTHY'S WORDS:

Some children who came to us were from tough situations and challenged with things from which our own children had been protected. Nearly every child we got was angry. They wouldn't have been in foster care if their parents had been in a situation to help them and teach them right. But they always loved their parents, I found.

We got children at all times of the day, in all weather and from all kinds of circumstances, even children who had been in jail.

Once a boy came from the funeral of his murdered mother. The thirteen-year-old boy had seen his father shoot and kill her right on their front porch. Roland was a big, handsome boy, of Hawaiian descent. He said his father worked for the railroad. He would get drunk and pass out. Roland and his mother would roll him over to get money out of his pockets for food.

His father had the habit of shooting at his mother's ankles, at cats, at the phone. That was how Roland had lived. While he was with us, he cried at night. Manuel would go sit with

27

him, comforting the boy who had never known a father's love, with his presence.

Roland was an angry boy. He would get mad and run off. We could understand that he needed some time, but foster children "belong" to the state. If he was gone over two hours, we would have to report it. We searched for him desperately to avoid this.

Manuel finally told him, "Roland, if you take off one more time, keep going because we're not going to be looking for you anymore."

It was a couple days later, but Roland took off again.

I told Manuel, "We're going to have to call the SRS (social services) and report him!" But I waited. It was summertime, and I went out to mow the yard to distract my worried mind.

Roland jumped down out of the tree, saying, "Here, I didn't run off. I'll finish mowing the yard."

Our rascally thief, Bobby, found a use for tall Roland. Bobby got him to lift him up to steal pop out of the top of the locker at the ice plant on their way home from school.

When he was seventeen, Roland got his girlfriend pregnant. She was from a nice family at our church—they gave the kids their blessing to get married.

Since his father had died in prison, there was no one but the state who had legal control over Roland. A judge had to give approval for the marriage since Roland was underage. He got a job as a welder and the couple moved out west eventually.

While I was working at Wal-Mart, I had a visitor.

"Hi, I'm Roland's son. My dad talked about you so much that I wanted to meet you."

The young man was going to Kansas University to become a doctor. I wasn't at all surprised. Roland had always been intelligent. I'm sure Manuel's fathering helped to shape Roland into a good dad to this fine young man.

1960s

Manuel was an instinctive parent, perhaps because of things he experienced as a young boy. He could discipline without a lot of words. There was one time when he taught our boys the consequences of disobedience without saying anything.

In order to save on money, Manuel learned to cut hair and bought a barber chair. Our two oldest sons, Daniel and Ron, grew their hair long like the Beatles, despite Manuel's and my preference.

That night, fifteen and sixteen-year-old Ron and Daniel were late for curfew. We had taught our kids not to miss curfew. The city's was midnight, and our family's was 11:30 p.m. However, 1:30 a.m. passed, and they still weren't home. I was worried, imagining car wrecks and such. I was relieved when I heard them come through the door.

I thought Manuel had fallen asleep beside me. But no. After a few minutes, Manuel got up calmly and went upstairs to the boys' room. He brought them down, holding their hands as if they were little boys. I stood in the doorway in my nightgown, waiting to see what would happen.

"You can go on back to bed now, Dorothy," said Manuel.

I didn't know what he was going to do. Then I heard the barber chair pumping up. I listened, anxiously. There was not one word spoken by my boys or my husband. Just the sound of the electric clippers.

In the morning, I saw the boys had a nice, short haircut.

Ron worked at a gas station and was so embarrassed by his lack of hair that he wore a stocking cap through the summer.

His boss asked why he wore it. Ron took off the cap and said, "We didn't obey the rules so Dad cut our hair."

IN RON'S WORDS:

I came to visit Mom and Dad one morning, and my conversation became about a problem with my teenage son. He wasn't minding. He was leaving my tools out, and I couldn't find them, etc. I was talking to Mom—Dad was reading the newspaper. His face was covered from view. As I was complaining about Mario, Dad started chuckling. I immediately shut up, because I realized Mario was just like me when I was his age—and this was payback time.

1980s
IN DOROTHY'S WORDS:

I was so glad that later I got to see Manuel in action as a teacher in his classroom, when I became a para-professional. His students were not easy; they had special needs. But they were our kind of people—we love special kids.

One day there were two boys who had been friends their whole lives, one husky, one tall and thin. For some reason, they got into a fight. I wondered what Manuel was going to do. The boys were standing poised to throw punches. Manuel just walked up between them without a word and the boys went back to their seats.

That's how Manuel functioned with our kids too. He was strict, but he was good with them. They knew he meant business.

"You're a soft touch," Manuel told me. "It takes two kinds, anyway."

We felt kids needed to be under control, but they also needed a lot of love. And our foster kids needed even more.

AT A PARK IN INDEPENDENCE, KANSAS ON TOP: SALLY AND RITA, FROM THE LEFT THELMA, CAROLINE AND CHRISTINE, MELISSA AND BLISS, MARTIN AND NICKY, KNEELING.)

March 31/April 1, 1979
HE FINDS TIME FOR 37 CHILDREN
by Marsha Woolery of the Parson Sun Staff

Like all dads, Manuel C. Perez is a busy man, but some-where between his special education classes at Parsons High School and board meetings for the Southeast Kansas Area Agency on Aging, he's made time for 37 children.

Only four are "biologically" his, he explained, but the others, ranging from a tiny black baby to a Japanese Labette Community Junior College student, have been just as much part of the family.

Perez, a native Parsonian of Mexican-American heritage, contends his pace of life is harassing and the days of teaching on average 11 special education students, coupled with the unpredictable nights at home, have so melted the months and years away that he has trouble remembering dates. He even reported his age as 57 before Dorothy, his wife, corrected him to say that he was only 55.

And how many children does the Perez household support now?

"We say eight before the phone rings," Mrs. Perez said. "It changes that quickly."

The couple's experience as foster parents for the last 16 years has been a sacrifice—of freedom, of days without crises and mostly just time for themselves.

But they relish the joy it's brought to their lives as they've watched their children grow into the community and become individuals in their own right.

Perez, who operates a plastering firm on the side with his son, Daniel, said, "It's kind of like plastering. You take the basic material and try to be creative with it. With the children, there's the nucleus of something there to begin with that you have to work through with the child until he finds his own individual ways."

He equates the satisfaction to that of a teacher's, only amplified with the proportionate extra pain and hours—counseling sessions until early morning, vindictive calls from natural parents and even visits from Parsons police wondering about stolen cars and the like.

But the Perez' proudly pull down dozens of portraits from the walls and easily tell one success story after another.

One boy, who saw his father shoot and kill his mother but lived through the hate and nightmares to finish school and become a welder. And a girl, who in the midst of a mentally retarded family, had "no worldly concept of what life in the practical sense was like," Perez noted. She is now married and has a son, named after Perez.

She and her six brothers and sisters were the first foster children the Perez' reared...The new children ushered in a whole different routine, or rather, an unroutine, to the Perez family.

"In a foster home setting," Perez explained, "it's traditional that you don't make any appointments, you don't make any schedules."

The priorities of the day—getting everyone up in the morning, gathering everyone to the dinner table and putting everyone back in bed at night—are regular. The rest of the day is left to run as it will.

With their first foster children, the problems and adjustments were compounded. The children couldn't tell time except by television shows, so that Mrs. Perez once found them in bed several hours early when a special election show came on. Thinking it was the news, they obediently went to bed.

Their mentally retarded (foster) children also spawned a whole new vocabulary for the Perez', so that dinner conversation now is still peppered with "please pass the cotty cheese, or the purghetti."

Through the years, the Perez home has grown from a small "shack" when the couple first bought it after their marriage in 1950, to a rambling white stucco with seven bedrooms.

"It was one addition after another," said Mrs. Perez. "Just like the kids—you never knew when another one was coming or what you were going to do with him."

Perez and his sons and other children have done most of the work on the expansion of their home. The physical work, he explained, gives him the daily sense of accomplishment that teaching at school and at home can't always provide.

Chores are mandatory for the Perez children, too, to give them practical skills, make them industrious and just keep the household running, the Perezes noted.

"I think the secret of our keeping an even keel," Perez said, "is that we all just have to live as the Perez family. We work as a family, eat as a family and are treated as a family."

Children are considered an integral part of the clan from their arrival, no matter how long they stay—"sometimes it's a day and sometimes it's a lifetime," Mrs. Perez said.

Outsiders are usually sincerely interested in the family, Perez said. Politely they will ask if the group is a "scout" troop, particularly on their summer camping trips which have taken them from the east coast to Mexico.

Although Perez professes that some day he'll "get off the merry-go-round," he doesn't appear to be moving that way just yet. Despite any initial reluctance, he's a man who finds it difficult to say no when he's needed.

As an example, he's been junior class sponsor at the high school for the last dozen years, just because no one else will do it. How does he do it all?

"You just hook on and hang in and go with the wind," he said.

1940s
IN MANUEL'S WORDS:

Jack Winslow and I had were close at Saint Patrick's school. I became friends with his family and enjoyed Mrs. Winslow's kindness.

Then, suddenly, I lost my friend Jack to the Neosho river. He and a friend went to the dam in a boat when it was at flood stage and Jack drowned. It was a tragedy for Mom and Dad Winslow.

It was through my relationship with the Winslows that Sister Dominico became one of my favorite people, along with her friend Sister Viola. It was wonderful to know Sister Dominico and Sister Viola. Working at Mercy Hospital was one of my first jobs, as a summer employee, doing janitorial duties. What a good experience, as I reflect on those memorable moments.

At Mercy Hospital, the head surgical nurse, Sister Anthony, was very influential in my acquaintance with my God.

On a couple of occasions, I was asked to drive the sisters to Wichita—a wonderful retreat for them and a learning experience for me. Along the way, there was chatter and laughter, and the telling of stories. For me, it was a time of prayer and meditation, a time of God's sharing and of serious thought—it was my privilege to be a part of it. It was also a time for me to learn that storytelling could be puritanical and clean, yet cause uproarious laughter.

In high school, I worked at a gas station in town. An ammunitions plant was being built in Parsons and I met a father and son from Minnesota working as carpenters on the project. They were looking for a place to stay and I, without asking anyone, let them stay there at the station. The son, Tom, and I became life-long friends. It was Tom's son, Kevin, whom our foster daughter Joan married years later.

CHAPTER FIVE

What We Leave Behind

1940s

IN DOROTHY'S WORDS:

My younger brothers, John and Leonard, and I walked two miles to school. My piano teacher lived part way in between. I took piano lessons from first grade through eighth grade, although I found my playing never matched that of Liberace!

I had to leave early in the morning to have my piano lesson and get to school on time. When it was still dark outside, I would get spooked and practically ran to my lessons.

Every year, Miss Simpson had a piano recital performed at church. I always did fine. Except the year I was in eighth grade. I got up on stage to play my song, which I knew well. But my first chord was absolutely sour.

My teacher was sitting in the front and whispered, "Try again, Dorothy." She repeated it and I kept trying.

But it got worse each time. I laid my head down on the keyboard and started crying. My mom had to come up on stage and get me. I left bawling.

When I got home, I sat down to try again and played my song just perfectly. I did go to lessons for another year, but when it came time for another recital, I wouldn't go. I think my dad may have wasted the money for my lessons.

We did keep the piano, and I was blessed with it after my marriage. What happened to it is a story for later.

I attended school in Liberty, from first grade until February 22, 1945. I remember that day quite well because I was a junior in high school, and it was George Washington's birthday. That was the day I had to leave Liberty and move to Parsons, KS. I cried all the way.

I was leaving my long-time friends and moving to this old farmhouse with no electricity, no running water and, you can probably guess, an outhouse. You would have cried too.

Earlier that year, my family had gone to Parsons to visit my aunt and uncle. The farm next to theirs was for sale, and my family bought it. My parents went back to Liberty to sell my dad's business and our home.

Later, my husband and I fostered children who had moved around a lot, who had lost not only friends, but their family, their belongings and their place in the world. My experience as a teen equipped me to truly feel their pain.

Different children reacted differently to these hardships. We weren't in Oz, but perhaps like the Tinman, Lion and Scarecrow, they were each looking for what they felt they lacked.

1970s

In the mid 1970s, thirteen-year-old twin sisters, Christine and Carolina, came to us along with their younger sister, Nicky. Their mother was in Osawatomie, a mental facility. A total of ten siblings had all been in foster care at some point. These were the three youngest.

THE TWINS AGE 13 AND NICKEY, AGE 10, IN 1974.

Carolina had been suspended from middle school for drugs. Since they came in March, she was out of school until September. So she was at home with me.

One Sunday, I told Carolina that she could not go off with her friends—she would go to church with the family. Instead, she cussed me out. That didn't exactly put me in the mood for worship.

I finally told the girls that we wouldn't listen to those words in our home—if they continued, the state would have to put them else-where. "It's up to you," I said. "Our home is yours, if you want to stay."

The girls chose to stay and went with us to church after that. The three girls became part of the family.

I always made the kids clothes. The twins didn't want to dress alike but Nicky and our daughter Melissa were the same age and wanted to wear matching clothes.

Dear Manuel and Dorothy,
I made this card just to show you how much I appreciate what you've done for me. Nope. This card tells you how much I love you both. Love ya, Nicky

The twins were on the first girl's basketball team at Parsons High School and Carolina became the homecoming queen. The girls stayed with us until they graduated high school and aged out of foster care. After graduation, we convinced Carolina to go to Pittsburg State College—we were proud that she graduated with her degree.

We kept in touch a little. We knew Christine had married and had a difficult time with her son. Carolina married a state trooper and became vice president of a bank. We were grieved to hear that Nicky passed away suddenly in her late thirties due to a blood clot.

The girls came to our 50th wedding anniversary party. Christine later wrote us this letter.

Dear Manuel and Dorothy,
I am sure I speak for Carolina and Nicky when I say that we can never thank you enough for all you did for us. I know we didn't seem very appreciative during our years with you, and that's because we never wanted to be there. But I am sure God put us there for a reason. That reason was because He knew we needed a good Christian home.

As I was sitting there at your celebration, I realized again what an impact your lives had on ours. I was proud to say that we lived with you and that your love for children and the Lord made me what I am today! Thanks for your dedication to children.

My first few years as an adult were pretty rough. I made a lot of mistakes, but God used those mistakes and He allowed me to see what I didn't want for my life. Through those trials, I was fortunate enough to find a good man who would love and honor me and also love my children.

I am very proud to tell you that I love teaching children, and I know that is one of my spiritual gifts. As you know, I worked at the state hospital for eleven years. After teaching (nursery at church) several months, I was asked to become a Coordinator for the Children's Ministry. I have been in that position for nearly four years now. I will brag about one more thing – I have been the Director of our Vacation Bible School program for the past two years. Serving is very exciting to me.

I say all these things so that you both will know that long ago you planted a seed in our lives and that seed has developed into a woman that loves the Lord with all her heart. My sister, Carolina, and her son were baptized this past fall, down at the lake. I have been praying for that for many years. I hope Nicky will be making that decision soon too.

Thank you for including us in your celebration and thank you for the Christian influence that you had on my life. I have one regret that the three of us haven't kept in touch more over the years.

Love,

Christine

Not every child we fostered has sent us a letter like that. Not every one of them has led a life of faith and service. But the way those girls changed blows my mind. I know that if we could help even one Tinman, Lion or Scarecrow to find their heart, their courage or their brain, it was worth it.

Christmas 1974

This year as they stand in line
    I count and see that there are nine!
    Some names remain the same,
    But there are new ones and I'll say them all by name:
Joan 19, Carol 17, Brian 16, Christine and Carolina 14 (twins), Martin 13, Nicky 10, Melissa 8 and Rita 7

This year has been a year for math. In other words, we have subtracted and added a few times. In one week, we minus-ed two and gained three. That's the way my math was all through school too. One year, we had four in kindergarten at once. This year, we had three birthdays on one day.

As of writing this, we now have up three Christmas trees. The little kids have done one, the big kids have done one, and I noticed a small decorated one upstairs in one of the bedrooms.

We did not take a lengthy trip this year. Guess the summer was mostly spent in gutting and completely remodeling an old house we bought a couple years ago for a rental property. Manuel really has so many ideas, and it is fun for us to watch the transformation as he brings something from nothing. With the help of the kids, I did completely paint the outside of that house. Since it is on a rather busy street, I became known about town as that "fat lady house painter."

We did go to Texas in July and the camp spot this year had plenty of water—in the lake, but no running water for necessary uses. On this trip, we learned that laundromats are useful for other uses than just dirty clothes! We would go late at night, when no one was about, and line them up for hair washing in the sink used for hand laundry. It worked great, even though to outsiders we probably would have looked like a tribe of gypsies just hitting town.

Danny, Rita C. and their baby, Lisa, live in Texas, and it is rather difficult for this grandma to have a grandbaby so far away.

Ron works for a carbon paper company here in town. He runs a press, but it is not a printing press.

Hope this letter finds you all well, and we send our greetings to each of you. "You can have that Christmas feeling all year if Christ is in your heart."

Even though, our house is not always tidy-usually messed-

We feel God has really blessed

And if in number we were only two

Manuel and I would really be blue.

Best wishes to all from the Manuel Perez Family.

CHAPTER SIX

Dorothy and Manuel in World War II

1940s
IN DOROTHY'S WORDS :
I was thirteen-years-old when the USA joined World War II after the Pearl Harbor attack. I came of age as the world boiled with war.

There in Liberty, there would be electricity black-outs. Our yard was lit by a nearby street lamp, so the whole neighborhood would come wait in the eerie light of our yard.

IN MANUEL'S WORDS:
The year must have been 1942, nearing the time of the Christmas Posadas celebration, welcoming the Christ Child. I was nineteen-years-old. One day, my dad asked me to kneel beside him. My brother Mike had already been drafted. Perhaps Dad feared that I too would be answering the call. I did as he bid. How thankful I am for Dad's action—I cherish his faith. Through this act, he passed on an inherent attitude that I should never feel alone, but with my faith, I should stand strong.

Later, my older brother Joe was drafted and served his country. Both Mike and Joe returned home safe. I cannot pretend that they returned with complete psycological fitness as they served in physical combat and lost comrades. It must have been devastating to take another's life, even in combat. However, self-preservation instinctively prevails.

The World War brought me pain from within with the loss of what might have been and the loss of childhood friends.

So many volunteered to serve and conscription called for those who were needed. Because of the gunshot wound to my abdomen, I was unable to serve in that same vein and did not qualify for active duty.

I did try to become one of that fraternity, and eager to serve, I dropped out of high school to volunteer for a civil service job.

As a civil employee, I served with the Air Service Command, at Hillfield in Ogden, Utah. The instructor of Mechanical Drawing was my ticket to the drafting department at the "Hill." I took my job as a Blueprint Tracer eagerly.

They pushed for perfection in modification of aircraft parts. The blueprint drawings were used as master copies for other repair units and used in the modification of propellers, motors, bomb sights. I can't recall why, but the wind tunnel was a magnet of my attention.

I recall each department worked at a feverish pitch in the process to make the aircraft air-worthy. The warbirds then returned to duty with up to date parts. Several of the planes were returned stateside to be used in war bond reviews.

It was interesting to visit Coordination—the walls were flush with demographic data in regards to aircraft operations and repair. The Conference room had graphs illustrating the various functions of the base.

At one point, I was fortunate to work on the assembly line of engine repairs from start to finish. Finally, the Pratt-Whitney was given a test, then picked for overseas shipment. I can only venture the thought of the "power plant" that kept the plane aloft and without this magnificent machine the plane was nothing. However, I don't dismiss the crew, for without their inherent wisdom the flying machine had no purpose.

My supervisor and military friend encouraged me to attend Weber College for algebra. Weber College whet my yearning to get back to school. Several of the staff encouraged me to complete my education. Along with this came advancement and the privilege of accompanying drafting personnel to the various departments to pick up modifications of the war-weary aircrafts.

My association with the military included the Navy and Marine base personnel in Clearfield, Utah, just across the way.

While in Ogden one Sunday, I was walking past a Catholic Cathedral. I marveled at the sound of music. To my amazement, the Italian POWs were singing the Mass a cappella. How beautiful were their voices! Enchanting. I did not attend Catholic services at that time, yet it was a sweet moment to recall my faith.

Years later, as I was able to watch a review of World War II war birds in Oskosh. I had read and heard much about this gathering place of warbirds, and I'd always wanted to pay my respects to the aircraft we put together, not to mention the casual acquaintances of the men and women who flew them.

I felt close again to those whom I had encountered on the Hill. These were special young men and women: theirs was an experience forever lasting for they received very few hours of flight training and yet were forced to fly by instinct.

It was good to hear the whine of the P51, the roar of the Pratt-Whitney, Navy Corsair, Hell Cat and many others of their vintage.

It was fascinating to once more observe the dynamic shape of Mother Earth—much of which had slipped away from memory. To my delight, I was called to remember the shadow cast by a high mound of earth.

It was good to hear the consistent roar of the motor, feel the air bumps, the lift of the craft, the gradual descent. To see the shadow of the high clouds casting dark areas on the terrain below. The fluffy white clouds as they blow their way across space.

I often reflect upon this poem.

High Flight by John Gillespie Magee (an American pilot with the Royal Canadian Air Force, killed at the age of nineteen on 11 December 1941).

"Oh, I have slipped the surly bonds of earth,
And danced the skies on laughter-silvered wings;
Sunward I've climbed and joined the tumbling mirth of
sun-split clouds -
and done a hundred things you have not dreamed of -
wheeled and soared and swung high in the sunlit silence.
Hovering there I've chased the shouting wind along
and flung my eager craft through footless halls of air.
Up, up the long delirious burning blue
I've topped the wind-swept heights with easy grace,
where never lark, or even eagle, flew;
and, while with silent, lifting mind I've trod
the high untrespassed sanctity of space,
put out my hand and touched the face of God."

In November of 1945, I returned home and completed high school at the age of twenty-two. I was never proud of having stopped my education, and didn't tell my children this until they had all graduated. However, I continued on and finished junior college in 1948 at age twenty-five.

CHAPTER SEVEN

A Bi-Cultural Couple

Late 1940s
IN DOROTHY'S WORDS:

DOROTHY, LOOKING LOVELY IN HEELS.

Even though the move from Liberty was very hard on me, I finished my high school career at Parsons High School and started

48

taking classes at Parsons Junior College where I met my future husband. I believe that was a reason for my move to Parsons.

My college Spanish teacher gave us an assignment to have a pen pal from a Spanish-speaking country. I got a boy from South America. The first letter I received was more than I could figure out. After all, I was just in my first semester of Spanish.

In my next class, a dark-haired boy, Manuel, sat across the aisle from me. I presumed he spoke Spanish. There were a number Mexican families in Parsons in the late 1940s, many employed by the railroad.

I had never spoken to him before. I poked him on the arm and asked if he could help me translate the letter. That was the beginning of our relationship. I'm not sure if Manuel wanted me to like him or was just interested in helping my grade, but he wrote most of my response letters for me. I never did become fluent in Spanish.

My business teacher at the college would start his class with two jokes. I usually didn't start laughing at the first one until he'd started on the second—it takes me a minute to get things sometimes!

"Meier, you will be a happy old woman," my teacher said to me. "Because you will just then be getting my jokes!"

After junior college, I moved to the YWCA in Parsons in 1948. The girls from farms out of town could live there, and our parents didn't worry as we had a house mother. I lived there so that I could work at my first job at First National Bank as a teller.

I had so much fun with the other ten girls there and made lifelong friends, including Lida Wood (later Overton). In our first building, there were meetings held downstairs, so we had to clear out right after supper and stay quiet upstairs—which was pretty hard for ten girls to do.

Later, about seven of us girls moved into a big apartment in a house. We would have card games and have outings with a group of boys who had cars. On the weekends, we'd all go back home.

DOROTHY AND MANUEL IN PITTSBURG WHILE DATING.

One summer, Manuel and his older brothers were plastering at the convent being built by the Cathedral of the Plains. Since he was carpooling, Manuel lent me his old telephone truck so I could get around town.

I would load up the girls, and we'd go to the drive-in movie or shopping. When Manuel got his truck back, he asked me, "Why do all the boys in town wave at me when I'm driving?" Seems that truck had gotten a reputation for being full of girls!

It was the late 1940s when we started talking about getting married. Not everyone thought love could come in different colors. A bi-racial marriage was uncommon then.

My dad was a stubborn old German and didn't like the idea of "inter-marriage." I'd say he was even furious.

Mother didn't care what race my husband was. Her theory was the world would not be happy until we were all one color anyway. She was more concerned that Manuel was Catholic. She wanted us to go to a marriage counselor. Mother thought it would help us through the difficulties we would face. I didn't think this was a bad idea.

We found a Christian counselor in Kansas City. We spent the whole day there, talking to him, together and separately. Like the crybaby I am, I'd cried throughout the conversations.

The counselor said our basic backgrounds were similar, other than our race. Manuel's father worked for the railroad for thirty-six years, while mine was a farmer. We had good middle-class compatibility on our side.

He felt the fact that Manuel was in college was important. Later, Manuel would be the first Mexican in Parsons to receive a Master's degree.

When alone with me, the counselor asked, "Are you aware that your children could be dark?"

I said, "I think little Mexican babies are beautiful! Little white babies aren't so pretty when they're first born, I don't think."

At the end of the day, we paid and headed home. Like the jokester that he was, Manuel said, "You know, we could have saved $10 and you could've just cried on my shoulder!"

A couple times Manuel tried to break up with me. Maybe it was his strong sense of family, honor and integrity. He said he didn't want my father to be angry with me. But we couldn't be apart from each other and always made up. We dated for five years.

My bank co-workers began asking when we would go ahead and get married. At a bank picnic, the bank president asked Manuel, "Are you planning on giving Dorothy a ring?"

Manuel said, "Eventually, but I can't until I'm out of school."

The bank president said they had a diamond as collateral on a debt, with only $40 left to pay on the bill. Manuel paid it, and I had an engagement ring. A jeweler later told us the diamond would be valued at $1,700.

We waited until he graduated with his bachelor's degree from Pittsburg State, in December 1950 and then were married. Actually, we eloped.

It was New Year's Eve and I was the first one back to the YWCA apartment after the weekend. Then Verna Lee, who wrote for the Parsons Sun, and Lee, who was the Sun photographer, arrived.

Lee asked, "So when are you and Manuel going to get married?" After all, we had been dating for years. When Manuel came, Lee told him, "We're getting you guys married. Tonight."

Verna Lee arranged everything. Since it was Sunday, the courthouse was closed. But while she was on the phone trying to find a place, the phone operator butted in on the line and said, "You can go to Huntsville, Arkansas!" It seems there was no waiting period for the certificate there. The operator called a justice of the peace to come in and marry us. I always wondered who that helpful person was!

Off we went to Arkansas. Verna Lee and Lee stood up as our witnesses, and he took all the pictures for us. One of these shows Manuel sitting in the car with me playfully pulling his arm, as if I was dragging him in to get married. We were both pretty thrilled, however.

LET'S GET MARRIED!

Meanwhile, all our friends were waiting on us for the New Year's Eve party and didn't know where we had been.

"We were busy getting married!" we told them. They didn't believe us, so we whipped out our new marriage certificate.

Later, we had a church wedding. However, my father still hadn't met Manuel and wouldn't speak to me until after a special event in 1952.

As Manuel couldn't start teaching until the following fall, he worked with his brother plastering. He used our only car to haul his tools.

I walked the two miles down the gravel road to my job at the bank. I knew exactly what time I had to leave to be on time. One morning, I noticed a house moving down the road towards me. It was going slow, as they had to lift electric lines and cut limbs. However, it was far enough down that I couldn't go down another street. It had rained the night before and the ditches were full. Without a cellphone, I couldn't call ahead to the bank to say I'd be late.

I decided to hunker down and crawled underneath the stopped house. A man on the roof was so surprised to see me come out the other side that he nearly fell off. I did make it to work on time and have often told the story of the house that almost ran me over.

Our friends, coworkers and classmates, were happy to see us married. Everybody loved Manuel. I've since learned of the prejudices that existed in our town then that I wasn't aware of.

We were the third bi-cultural couple in town at that time. Manuel's family friend John married a blonde girl, Stella, who later became my dear friend. Then an English girl came as a war bride.

I could never have known back when we were dating that our bi-cultural family would bring many wonderful, yet hard-to-place children into our home.

1990s

In 1992, five-year-old Johnny was our last foster child, a handsome boy from a Caucasian mother and African-American father. Johnny had been beaten as baby for crying. He was taken from the home when he was eighteen-months-old. Social Services gave the mother the choice between staying with her boyfriend and keeping her baby...and unfortunately, she didn't choose her son.

We were Johnny's sixth foster home. He had already been suspended from kindergarten—I didn't even know that could happen. He was already seeing a psychiatrist. Because he needed continuing therapy, we decided not to switch and drove him back to Newton to see his psychiatrist.

The doctor shared with us that he believed the root of the problems was the abuse and lack of love shown to Johnny as a baby. "He was hit when he was a crying baby," the psychiatrist told me. "He'll be crying out all his life."

Since he was bi-racial, Johnny had curly hair, but his skin was the same tone as my Mexican boys. One summer morning, he came down stairs. I screamed.

"Everyone says I'm black, so I guess I might as well be black," said Johnny.

He had covered his skin with black wax shoe polish. It took me all day to scrub it off of him—he turned pink! I should have taken a picture. What a sight.

Johnny was especially close to our oldest son, Daniel. He would follow Daniel around like a puppy as he worked. Daniel was going to adopt him, and Johnny was so happy. But Johnny kept getting into trouble, and that dream never became a reality.

From Johnny's notebook, 1995-1996:

My favorite game in the fall is basketball. I'd like to be a professional basketball player in the NBA on the team of Orlando Magic and be like Anfernee Hardaway and Shaq put together. (Note written on the bottom by Manuel: Set your goals and strive to meet them, and you will succeed. Remember school. To do well in school because that is the path for the NBA. They usually recruit from college. You can accomplish lots. Go for it.)

<u>Loving</u> is a feeling you show and feel. I feel loving of my kittens cause their fur is soft and cosy.

<u>Guilty</u> is a way you feel like when you know you did it and you take the blame. When I was not doing good in school, I was guilty about not doing good like not completing my work and messing around. Yeah, I was guilty cause it wasn't anyone 'sep me. Now things are going better I turned my act and my work around, now I do my work and use my time wisely.

<u>Jealous</u> is a way you feel when someone is doing better or doing something you wish you could do or do better than that someone. I was jealous because my friends had money and I didn't. So now I get money by asking or doing chores and cleaning the house.

10-30-95

Friday morning when I was on my way down to the bus stop, I smelled a weird smell. So I told my mom, and she smelled it too. After school and I noticed our garage was caught on fire about around 10:00 and my mom said some of the kittens died and at that moment it felt like my life was getting farther down the drain. It felt sad and angry and at that moment I was both of those feelings that really hurt.

11-6-95

The good day will be when Troy (social worker) can't touch me. When I go to Daniel's, I want it to be the best thing that happened to me.

11-13-95

My brother (Daniel) is getting married on December 2. After I get adopted, I will have a mom and dad. I've never had a permanent home before. This will be the first time maybe to be in a permanent home. My brother is marrying Debi, and she is very friendly. I hope she will be my mom and Daniel will be my dad. I hope I get to help with the wedding.

3-5-96
My favorite pet is Simba and Bubba. They are my dogs, and why, because when I feel sad they know how I'm feeling so they cuddle up close to me and then start licking me and I give them a great big hug.

On his twelfth birthday, in 1996, Johnny was arrested. He and a friend had gone bike-riding in our quiet neighborhood. It wasn't long before a police officer brought a sobbing Johnny back to me.

The boys had gone into a house and peed on someone's bed. In another house, they had poured pop on a computer. By then, the police officers had been called—they caught Johnny climbing in the window of the third home.

Here's where I'll say that we had some wonderful social workers and a couple not-so-great ones. One of my favorite was an African-American woman, who appreciated that we never said no. However, I didn't appreciate Johnny's social worker and I don't think social work was his calling. He really didn't like Johnny. For one thing, Johnny was always creating problems.

By the time Johnny was arrested, I think the foster system was tired of fiddling with him. I've wondered if Johnny couldn't have stayed with us if a social worker had fought for him. Poor Johnny was sent to juvenile detention in Topeka, even though he was almost too young to be there. I feel it was easier for Troy to send him there than to bring him back to us.

We would all drive up to visit Johnny. One time we arrived as he got back from school—I remember how it bothered him that we saw the officers frisk him as he returned. He looked so shy and hurt. He knew he had done wrong, but couldn't get out of the cycle of self-destruction.

And once he was in the system, we couldn't get him back. While he was in Topeka, another family began to visit him. They adopted our Johnny, while he was still in juvie. The father would come on days we were visiting and spend all day. I thought they were a strange family—I wasn't impressed with them. They had already adopted a bunch of kids—I suspected there was something fishy there.

He was never happy in his adopted home. When I called, they would yell for Johnny to get off the phone, or they would listen to our conversation on the other phone.

While he was living with his adoptive family, he stole a small item from a store and was caught. Johnny listed us as his parents on the police report. We received a notification to come to his court session. I always got the impression that he did not like that family. I don't know if they were unkind or what.

When he was of age, Johnny went on his own and was in and out of trouble. When he was in prison in Oswego, we'd go to visit him. Every time he writes, he doesn't use his adopted surname, but his own.

I just loved him. He was one child that I wanted to change, to save.

Even looking back through letters he sent, brings tears to my eyes. Now in his late twenties, he has been in and out of jail. It's not every mother who is happy to get a birthday collect call from prison, but I'll take what I can get, even if I have to pay for it.

Here's parts of letters he sent in May of 2004 while in prison.

"I'm gonna try my best from now on to do anything and everything to complete this program. Yeah, my social worker would hate to see me succeed. I'd love to throw it in his face also. He really did a number on me, moving me around, trying to show how much authority he had. I really don't care, is he still a social worker for the S.R.S. or what?

To tell you the truth, I don't know if I can live in Parsons from what the judge said back in 1996. Didn't he say I was kicked out of Parsons? I don't remember exactly how it went, but it wasn't good. They treated me like I was sixteen or so, and I just turned twelve.

But I did take that beebee gun to school in fifth grade. I also got kicked out a few too many times, fighting, not doing what I was supposed to do, yelling at teachers...

...Well, I got another "class one write-up" tonight, for laughing pretty much. So pretty much I'm on my last string, not to mention I've got four write-ups to face as it is. I think this program is twisted. They are supposed to scare you to where you want to straighten up, but instead they bring you down and set you up for failure.

I'm sorry to disappoint you...I don't like giving up, but I feel it is for my own good. I swear this program is a messed up one. KDOC gets anything they want pretty much, we barely get anything and that's a minimum prison like thing.

Anyways, I appreciate the concern, but to tell you the truth my social worker will never win. I'm still alive and young. I'll let you know the details when I find out what's gonna happen.

September 2004

These next three weeks are gonna be a killa for me. I'm gonna be so anxious to get on that bus headed to Parsons and chill, talk 'bout the good ol' days and what

I've been through since I left the day before my birthday (12th).

I can't wait to start doing carpentry work again. It's been too long since I got taught the ropes and doing what little I could with Martin, Daniel and Dad. To this day, that is still one of my favorite things to do, remodel and build things.

Do you guys still have that little wooden airplane I made out of scraps? Does Daniel still have the tools I used to keep in that little shed? Well, I'll be seeing you real soon, sooner than you'll notice, till then, take care.
Truly Yours, Your Son, Johnny

IN DOROTHY'S WORDS:

I haven't heard from him since he got out of prison in 2013. Johnny called Daniel, who said he'd be happy to give Johnny work. But we haven't heard since.

When he was little, Johnny would get despondent and go tinker in the garage. One time, he tore Manuel's white plastering pants up and nailed them to an old board. He painted "I Heart You Mom." That means a lot coming from a foster child, who just hadn't gotten love like they were supposed to.

Not every story has a happy ending. Not every child receives magic ruby slippers and clicks their heels to go to their forever home. But I was determined to love them and make their stay in this Dorothy's Kansas home meaningful.

THIS PICTURE WAS TAKEN BY THE PARSONS SUN ON MOTHER'S DAY WITH AN ARTICLE TALKING ABOUT THE MANY CHILDREN WHO CALL ME MOTHER. IN IT ARE OUR FIRST FOSTER CHILD, JOAN, AND OUR LAST FOSTER CHILD, JOHNNY. BACK ROW: RONALD, RITA, JOAN, DOROTHY, MARTIN, GREG, MINORU FRONT ROW: ZACK, JOHNNY, JADE AND JORDAN, MANUEL

CHAPTER EIGHT

No One is Divorced from This Family

1950s

IN DOROTHY'S WORDS:

DANIEL:

I was working at the bank right up until our first born, Daniel, was born in February 1952. My coworker Helen hadn't had a baby before, but she said, "You're making me nervous."

"I'm not even in pain," I assured her. There was something happening every five minutes, however. Finally, at my lunch hour, they convinced me to go to the hospital.

"Ok," I said. "But we'll have to stop at the dime store for some bloomers." Without nice, modern maternity wear, I was wearing a pair of boxers and was too embarrassed to let anyone see that. Also, there was another problem. I didn't know how to get ahold of Manuel.

He had graduated from college in December and wouldn't teach until the following fall, so he was plastering with his family's business.

At the hospital, Helen told the nurses that I wasn't hurting and that I was wearing boxers. "It's ok, honey, we see everything," they assured.

Helen got a hold of Manuel, who arrived with a joke. "I didn't know they made deliveries on Mondays!" He stayed with me for labor. The doctor said he'd have time to go home to milk the cow and feed the chickens, our "girls." When he came back, I asked Manuel if he'd written down how many eggs the girls had laid, to the doctor's confusion.

My mother came while I was in labor too. She was so excited that she pressed $10 into my hand. "It's from your father, for the baby," she said. He still hadn't met my husband or spoken to me.

After Daniel was born, the doctor was still working on me.

"What are you doing down there now?" I asked, embarrassing Manuel to death.

"Well, we need to do a few stitches," replied the doctor.

Manuel told me later that I asked the doctor what size of thread he used. I told him I used size 50. I just kept rambling on and on.

I loved having babies. And it was that baby that finally broke my dad down.

From Daniel's birth in February to August, Dad would bring Mom over every Wednesday night. He wouldn't come in or anything—he'd just drop her off and pick her up while he was at the stockyards.

One August evening, I waited and walked over to his truck before he could drive off. "Dad, I want you to meet your grandson."

That's all it took. He came inside. Dad really loved Manuel once he met him. He was a good grandfather too. A favorite memory is him dressing up in a Santa suit to surprise the boys.

Cultural differences in handling family conflicts still amaze me—how can one choose rejection over love? We surprised a young Japanese boy, who had experienced rejection in his family.

FROM TOP LEFT: JOAN, RON, BOBBY, DANIEL, BRIAN, MINORU,
FRONT ROW LEFT: RITA, TEDDY AND MANUEL, HAROLD
AND DOROTHY, MARTIN AND MELISSA ON THE STAIRS.

1970s

It was June of 1972, and I received a call from the local college. It was a plea for help with an exchange student, Minoru from Japan. He had come too late in the year for the summer session and too early for the fall. They had placed him with an elderly lady as a host who lived close to the college.

Minoru had had seven years of English studies but never had much opportunity to use it. He and his host struggled to communicate, the man from the school explained to me.

We couldn't communicate with him any better, but the school administrator knew we had a house full of stray puppies/children and he figured Minoru could build his confidence in the language by playing with the kids.

"If Minoru can stay with you for the summer," he said, "we'll find him a home closer to the college."

"Why not," I said. Just another experience for us. Our motto has always been "room for one more."

Minoru came that same day, adding to the company we had from St. Louis. He had enough baggage for his two-year-stay. His mother had even sent a special pan for cooking his rice—the whitest rice I have ever seen. She sent him more rice regularly.

The kids were so excited to have him here, even our friends' children. They all filled our front room to welcome him. One of the boys told Minoru, "The boys sleep upstairs." Our foster son, Roland, offered to help with the baggage.

Minoru stood up straight, bowed with his whole body and said, "Thank you." He sat back down very politely. It took a couple more times of doing this before Roland just motioned for him to follow and headed up the stairs.

We all trailed behind and watched him unload his clothes. He had a brand new suit with the tags still on it. As he put it on the rack, he said, "Suit for wedding."

Minoru's famous words were, "I do not understand." He didn't know why all these kids called me "Mom" but had different last names. On Sunday afternoons, we would go down to Oswega jail after church to visit Bobby, our car thief. Minoru would go along with us, but on the way home, he said, "I do not understand."

"What do you not understand?" I asked.

He shared that he had come to the US in part because his brother had done something wrong and he had been divorced from the family. In his culture, you didn't go visit them and continue to treat them like family.

It was an enjoyable summer, and Minoru helped around the house. He was very quick in his actions. He started doing the dishes without being asked. As it was a hot summer, he would get all sweaty as he washed them.

By fall, Minoru said, "If I buy a bicycle to go to school, can I keep on staying here?"

We were happy to have him stay. Manuel always joked with Minoru. Manuel would show him an object that said "made in Japan" and then say, "I think I'll turn you over and see if it says 'made in Japan' on you." They had a good laugh.

At Christmas that year, Manuel gave me a dishwasher. When he rolled it in, it was Minoru that ran over and hugged him.

Christmas Letter 1972

Dear Ones,

All the stockings were hung—well they were all up and as I turned my head a moment ago, Harold had taken one down and had it on his foot!

This is the age of instant everything—instant pudding, instant potatoes and even instant kids, and this is our way of announcing new members of our family. We are back in the terrible twos, and his name is Harold.

Two days before we took our vacation this summer, a phone call came at noon whereby a home was needed for two brothers, age two and five. The five-year-old is Benny. They arrived three hours later, and life has been more lively than ever.

Benny's birthday was the day after their arrival and also the same day as Martin's, so we had a huge party. The following day, we packed extra duds in the car and headed for St. Louis for several days.

Not only did we get instant little kids this year, but in June, the junior college called and they needed a place for a foreign exchange student. The Far East has been added to our hacienda, and his name is Minoru

Makita from Tokyo and he is such an interesting boy. He is a freshman, and he intrigues us all.

At first, we used sign language and thumbed constantly through a Japanese-English dictionary. His English has improved, but our Japanese remains the same! We made his Christmas stocking today, and he put his name on it with Japanese symbols. It was quite outstanding among the others.

In fact, this summer was an international summer for us as we were so fortunate to host a teacher from Essen, Germany in our home for several days. This was a few weeks after Minoru's arrival. With his English in the beginning stages and Hildegard's half-German and half-English sentences and Manuel's teasing them both in Spanish, it was like having a house full of magpies.

Hildegard came to our home through the American Host program, whereby American families open their homes to European teachers, and the European teachers learn the typical American way of life. I fear poor Hildegard went back with a misunderstanding of the American way of life as our household is like "confusionville." We certainly enjoyed her visit, and we certainly hope we can visit both Germany and Japan someday. How great that would be.

Both Dan and Ron are working back in Parsons again—good to have them around. Even though working away from home was a great experience for both of them. Brian and Martin are still on the paper route, the one we have had since Danny started it. They have Melissa, age six now, deliver a few papers every evening. I guess this is why the neighbor lady told me one day that her boy never would get a chance at the route as we had so many to inherit it. Guess she was right as her boy is sixteen now, and we still have a few more to grow up to the paper route.

Joan is my right-hand gal—without her I wouldn't accomplish the things I have to do in each day. She finishes school this year. Bobby seems to be Manuel's good helper.

We have done some more property buying this year. They better stop having these Sheriff's sales, as we can't seem to resist them. These sales are quite an adventure, and one ends up with good bargains sometimes. Our last purchase was five acres with an old beat-up house and a leaning barn. The barn, we will tear down, but Dan, Bill and Manuel are completely rewiring, plumbing and revamping the house in general. It will be nice soon. We hope the boys are learning some of these skills so they can maintain or build a house someday.

Rita is five now and in school. She and Benny are three weeks apart in age, so both are in the same kindergarten class. Seems strange to have two kids age five, but they don't look anything like twins!

Once a year, I turn author and since I only write letters once a year, I find it hard to turn myself off. Even though I say, "I, I, I" throughout my letters, the thoughts are from all of us. Manuel, I and all the children wish you the best.

May God bless your home and those you love
In countless different ways
At this whole Christmas season
And throughout the coming days.
Merry Christmas from the Perez Family

One evening, Minoru attended a dinner at Pittsburg State for young exchange students. He met a Japanese girl, Michiko,

68

who was attending the university there. Minoru started going over to see her frequently, but he'd always come home saying, "She's so bossy."

"Well, why do you keep going over there?" I asked.

"Because she speaks Japanese," Minoru said, with a shrug.

He graduated from Parsons junior college in May and was planning to go to Pittsburg State the next year. Several of the other Japanese students went to work in Chicago at a big Japanese restaurant for the summer—Minoru and his "bossy" Michiko went too.

In August, Minoru called me and said, "Get ready for a wedding."

"Whose wedding?" I asked, a bit confused.

"Mine."

I said, "Well, who are you marrying?"

"Michiko!"

As a mother, I had to ask. "Isn't that the girl you said was too bossy?"

Minoru said, "Well, things change."

During the wedding rehearsal, excitement increased and the language went to Japanese, leaving the minister just as confused as they. They were married on my birthday, August 25, in our church. Minoru wore his "suit for wedding."

Manuel and I were witnesses at their wedding. We felt this quite an honor. The reception was held at our home.

Wedding Announcement Parsons Sun
Miss Kanbara, Makita Married Here August 25

The Westside Christian Church was the setting for the wedding of Michiko Kanbara and Minoru Makita on Aug. 25. The Rev. Albert Delbridge preformed the ceremony.

The bride is a native of Kobe, Japan, studying at Kansas State College in Pittsburg. Makita, also a native of Japan, has lived with the Manuel C. Perez family for the past two years.

The bridal couple was attended by Mr. and Mrs. James Mount of Parsons and Mr. and Mrs. Perez.

The bride wore a formal gown of blue with white lace trim. She wore a shoulder-length veil held by a white embroidered caplet and wore a corsage of pink carnations.

Mrs. Georgia Meier and Mrs. Carl Merman assisted at a reception in the Perez home.

The bride is a graduate student at KSCP. The bridegroom is a 1974 graduate of Labette Community Junior College in Parsons and is attending KSCP, majoring in speech and drama.

The couple is at home in Pittsburg.

Minoru, his wife, and their three beautiful girls now live in Dallas, Texas, but they are still a part of our family. Minoru came to Manuel's funeral and spoke about his American father at the cemetery.

I hope we demonstrated unconditional love to Minoru while he was with us. Perhaps we learned that through my father's rejection and then his renewed love.

Here's a sweet letter Manuel wrote to our daughter-in-law, Rita C as we called her, and grandchildren after she and Daniel divorced. Daniel moved to Florida, but we kept the little grandkids under our wing. Things happen in life that hurt and we can't always understand what happened. Rita C. knows we love her still.

Fall 1989
Rita C., Lisa, Sarah, Jeremiah,

There are so many things, ideas, moments of inspiration I've wished to share.

Each of you are dear to me. Sometimes I'm sure you have wondered, "who cares?" But I ask, have you given thought to your options. It's tough going alone – but you are not alone. The spirit of us – our relationships – we are there.

Do not fail to seek us out – for it is then that you will truly find the depth of our love. Yet you must be the one to know how steadfast your faith is – unto yourself.

Let not the material world intervene – the mortals around you cause you to waiver. Do not compromise.

Make your life count for that which you desire. But do search diligently to know that which you desire is possible through your sincere efforts.

My mom and dad, your granddad and grandmom, only gave me their moral support. Their worldly knowledge of what the future might hold was beyond their reach.

Yet, from their faith and love, came the realization that I could make a difference in their life. But it was I and only I that made that difference. How fortunate to have had the faith of God to guide me for their sake and Him.

Manuel

CHAPTER NINE

Birth Children

1950s

IN DOROTHY'S WORDS :

I was the oldest of three children. My mother's sisters in Lindsborg had large families. It was just always my dream since early childhood to have many children. Manuel and I did get off to a good start, I thought, with our four boys.

RON, MARTIN, BRIAN AND DANIEL WITH MANUEL
IN SWEATERS DOROTHY KNITTED.

RON:

When I went into labor with our second son, Ronald, things were progressing quickly. We were on our way to the hospital, when Manuel pulled over at a drug store. I wasn't sure what he was doing.

Our friend Lee, who had helped us elope, pulled up beside the car. He and his wife had seen our car and wondered if we wanted to go play cards.

"If Manuel ever comes out of this drugstore, I'm going to go have this baby!" I said.

Manuel finally came, and we made it to the hospital. While in labor, I looked up at Manuel who was standing at the mirror, shaving.

"What are you doing?" I asked.

"Our child can't see me this way," he said. "I have to get my face right for the baby." And that's what he had gone into the drugstore for—a razor. We named little Ronald Lee after our dear friend.

Ron has always been my jokester. Not long ago, we were going to our family's favorite restaurant, Chicken Mary's in Pittsburg. Ron came around to help me out of the car while everyone else went inside the restaurant.

"Tell them there'll be two more in about thirty minutes," he called. At eighty-six-years-old, I guess I'm not moving as quickly!

Ron and Sonia were married in 1981. Their courtship was interesting because Sonia is from Mexico.They met when through some of our renters. They were here from Mexico working on a sewer line in town. Ron became friends with them. Two years later, they asked if Ron would drive them to Mexico, if they paid for the gas. So Ron went to Mexico.

Sonia was the daughter of their next-door neighbor. Ron was very interested in her, and the letter writing began. He had to learn Spanish! The telephone calls became frequent and then as

Ron could, he'd go to Mexico to see her. The kids and I tried to learn Spanish while Sonia did a good job of learning English.

Ron and Sonia have Mario and Selena, our Spanish-speaking grandchildren.

After Ron was born, I miscarried. Such heartbreak. I was out hanging up clothes and miscarried at three months along. That tiny little baby was born so easily, without pain. I had to call for a neighbor lady to come help me—she took me to the hospital. I hemorrhaghed badly with that baby.

BRIAN:

In 1958 when I was pregnant with our third born, Manuel was going to Kansas University as Pittsburg didn't have all the hours he needed for his Master's degree in Special Education. Manuel would leave early Monday morning to arrive in time for his first class. He would spend the week there and be home Friday evening.

We had a neighbor across the road with pigs, cows, chickens, cats and dogs that ran wild. I suspect their children were starved. The animals roamed over into our yard looking for food. When I could, I would gather up the dogs and put them in our shed.

Manuel had an old telephone company truck with an enclosed metal bed, so Manuel would deliver the dogs on his way to Lawrence. He told his carpool fellow, "I brought company with me."

They always stopped at a coffee shop for a break. When Manuel opened the door, six dogs leaped out of the back. The fellow was shocked—and so was a policeman in his car across the street. They didn't stay for coffee that day but left, hoping the policeman wouldn't follow and ticket them.

While Manuel was still traveling back and forth for school, one Friday in November I had my doctor's appointment. Doctor Martin said, "Your baby will be here before this night is over!"

It happened that this was the night that my brother Leonard was to make his first solo cross-country flight for the Navy, from California to the naval base in Olathe. He wanted Mom and Dad to see him land.

This presented a logistical problem. Of course, Mom thought she shouldn't leave me, because Manuel wouldn't get back until about 9:00 p.m. Manuel's younger sister Lola was with me and could take me to the hospital in case he didn't make it in time.

I convinced Mom to go with Dad. "It will be the doctor delivering the baby anyway!"

It all went well. Manuel got home in time to leave his suitcase at the house and pick up mine.

Mom and Dad got home around midnight from Olathe, so Mom called the hospital to see if the baby had been born. At Mercy Hospital, they didn't have phones in the room yet. The nurse told her it was another boy. When the nurse came to see me, she said, "I don't know what your mother meant, but she said 'I guess Leonard brought the stork.'"

Because it was Thanksgiving weekend, Manuel got to stay home a whole week with us. He washed diapers and hung them out to freeze dry.

It was on Brian's birthday a few years later that President Kennedy was assassinated. I was making the birthday cake but never got it iced because we were all listening to the news.

Brian grew up to be my tender "Indian chief." He has a big heart, yet keeps to himself, even while living here with me, so we don't always understand what he is thinking or feeling. He works hard at the family plaster trade.

Letters from Manuel – Christmas 1991

Dear Son Brian,

It's not like you to keep this distance. Much like the lyrics of a song, "I know someone is thinking of me 'neath the canopy of blue."

Personally you don't really know how I've wished for your presence. Yes, we've met on the street—how fleeting those moments are.

Your kind acts are not forgotten. Yet they serve to give me notice that you care—a mannerism I've thought is much like you.

Each of you have given me a sense of pride—I can only guess that you don't realize that for me "time is fleeting." How I wish there was some way of causing a pause to savor the joy you bring.

As for me, I must accept my own faults, and yet, be accepting of the life styles of each of you. I cannot hold a grudge or will I.

Surely you each must recognize that our total make up is not alike. Dream on—don't stop for regrets—move on—meet the challenge for the future.

What's the good of having parents but that they prepare the way for their children and children's children?

I can't tell you how much today I cherish the gift of a loving dad, mom, brother and sister so much that their memory and spiritual love has made my life a joy to have shared a life with them. Guess it was the manner in which they personified love and sharing with others. Christ was born in Bethlehem.

Brian, you are a chip off the ole block. Your Uncle Joe has touched you and has graced you with your creative talent. You've made him proud with your workmanship.

He's not here, but spiritually I must thank you for him. You've been an inspiration as I've observed your house grow with you.

As head of this family, I care, I love, I cherish. I'm proud of each of you, regardless of what I see or think. Before you lay me to rest, I would be proud to know of your self-control.

Bless you,

Dad

KEITH:

After Brian, I was pregnant and made it to five months gestation, but that little boy, Keith Wayne, was stillborn. His obituary appeared in the newspaper. I'd been home from the hospital a few days when I got a call. It was from Stella, a woman I knew a little as our Mexican husbands had grown up together. Stella carried five babies to full-term and delivered them stillborn because of her RH factor—in those days, they didn't know what to do about it.

Stella called because she had seen the obituary. "I know how you are feeling right now. If you feel like talking, just talk."

We became very close because of our losses. Stella and I called ourselves the Blonde Mexicans. She called me Darby too because I was like the leprechaun always followed by little people.

Stella was a wonderful, strong person. When she was seventeen, she was in a horrible car wreck. She regained consciousness and found herself leaning against a tree, looking at her severed left arm on the ground. It was a miracle that she survived. She grew up thinking no one would ever want to marry her, but our friend John did.

Stella did everything with one arm, even roll tortillas. She would lay babies on a bed to change their diapers, with her knee holding them down and diaper pins sticking in the mattress. I was so proud of her.

Her last baby, Jody, they induced labor at seven months, as they thought there would be a better chance of her survival. There was also a good chance she'd be mentally retarded. Until Jody was four-years-old, they thought she was retarded as she functioned differently. Then they realized she was deaf.

Stella and John moved to St. Louis to be near a school for the deaf for Jody to learn to sign. We would pack up our kids, see them and go to Six Flags together, or they would come to visit Parsons. One time, Stella said, "Dorothy, watch. Jody will show you how she signs your name."

Jody's fingers formed a "d" by the side of her face, then spiraled out in crazy circles. "Jody thinks I'm goofy, huh?" I said with a laugh.

"No," said Stella. "You're Dorothy from Kansas. It's a tornado!"

Years later, Stella called me. "Dorothy, I know that God is still with me."

"I know He is," I said, wondering what was coming next.

"I have breast cancer," said my friend.

Since she couldn't drive herself to treatments, and John was working in the city, a neighbor boy would drive her. He would play around, bow in front of her and say, "Come on, Miss Daisy" as he was African American. Stella passed away from the cancer.

1961
MARTIN:

After the still birth, I had another miscarriage and a painful blood clot that sent me back to the hospital. When I was pregnant again, it progressed, and I grew more and more humongous. After all I had been through, I was afraid during all those nine months of pregnancy. I was afraid that I'd deliver, and the baby wouldn't survive.

Of course, we didn't know the gender in those days. Dr. Martin delivered the baby and then announced, "Well, Dorothy, you're not going to get out of being a den mother." It was another boy. We named him after Dr. Martin.

Martin grew up and married Shelley. They have three girls: Rachelle, Lauren and Marlee. I think Marlee's name is cute as it is a combination of Martin's name and the last part of Shelley's.

After Martin was born, the doctor told me that I shouldn't be pregnant anymore. My deliveries went well, but I hemorrhaged so badly.

That was hard to take, but I wasn't giving up my dream of having a large family, or at least of having a girl. "Can you help me?" I asked the doctor. I thought it might help with an adoption agency if he could verify that it was against medical advice for me to have more children biologically.

"I'd be glad to help if I can," said Dr. Martin.

Letter from Manuel

Martin,

Uncle Joe would and is most proud. You've been guided by his hand. Thanks for bringing this about in your home that you've provided for Shelley and the girls. You personify him well.

Personally, I'm proud in your craftsmanship and creativeness in your home.

Ron, Martin, Daniel,

As you fly in the openness of space, be aware that I share much of the feeling of being aloft. Do be careful and use judgment in bringing your bird home safely.

Ron, Martin, Brian, Daniel,

Each of you are excellent self-starters. I've watched you pick up the pieces as bad judgment appears in the form of reality. Your creativeness has been observed and not without recognition. Thanks.

CHAPTER TEN

Adopted Children

IN MANUEL'S WORDS: How precious life is when the dawn of life is just beginning within.

1960s
IN DOROTHY'S WORDS:
I figured there must be something I could do. Manuel knew I wanted a girl, and he was open to finding an alternative.

In July 1964, I went to the local Social and Rehabilitation Services (now the Department for Children and Families). When I said that I wanted to adopt, the man told me that we had too many children and thirty-six years-old was too old to adopt.

"Would you consider fostercare?"

"No," I said. "I want to keep my kids." I walked away, broken-hearted and crying.

We did start fostering after all, with the seven Nelson kids. I still wanted a baby girl, though.

I had heard of the Kansas Children's Service League (KCSL) in Wichita. I started composing a letter. I told the KCSL about my dream and desire. I was afraid they would say I had enough kids. I might have begged and implored.

The social worker later told me that they had passed the letter around the office, incredulous that with a house full of kids, I wanted a baby.

MELISSA IN GRADE SCHOOL

MELISSA:

Four months later, we were blessed with two-month-old Melissa. As we had asked for a little Latina baby, I think the process went faster. It's a sad fact, but because of prejudice of the time, Hispanic and black children weren't adopted as readily, I think. Melissa has a Mexican-Serbian heritage.

Usually, the Kansas Children's Service League in Wichita brings the family to a "baby room" to meet their new little one. Because there were so many of us, inlcuding the Nelsons, they

81

placed tiny Melissa in the middle of the board of directors' table. We all walked around it to see her.

I was concerned because I had given birth to my other babies—would I feel the same motherly connection to an adopted baby? From the moment the agency put our new baby in my arms, it was utter joy. No difference.

I loved making pretty little dresses for her. When Melissa was about three-years-old, she got into my sewing and shredded one of them. She cut the skirt into strips! To teach her the consequence of her action, I took her to the store in it, hoping there would be some embarrassment or remorse. Well, it embarrassed me more than her, but she never cut up another dress. I have a cute picture of her in that dress.

When she was in school, Melissa was always racing out to the bus. It couldn't get down our drive, so it would wait for them at the corner. I can see her running helter-skelter with only one shoe on, the other in her hand.

Rita would already be on the bus, but Melissa would be doing her hair and makeup, and she'd miss it. Then Manuel would have to drive her to school before going to teach his class.

One day, he said, "We're going to do this differently. You can't stay at home, but I can't keep driving you. If you miss the bus, you'll have to come to my classroom."

Melissa had to go with him several times. He would be teaching his special needs kids, ask a question and it would be Melissa who raised her hand to answer.

"You're not here to answer the questions!" Manuel told her.

Later, when there was friction at times between Melissa and me, Manuel had her walk the two blocks from the bus stop to spend time with him in his classroom. They were always very close.

1980s

IN MELISSA'S WORDS:

During my turbulent teenage years, Mom and I did not always see eye to eye. So my Dad's way of handling this was to try to minimize the time that Mom and I were home without his presence.

I attended Labette County High School in Altamont, and Dad taught at Parsons High School. The plan was for me to get off the bus on 32nd Street at the end of my school day. I would walk to PHS and sit with Dad in his classroom.

It was the end of his day, and he would grade papers and do lesson plans. It would basically end up being my own quiet time with Dad. I had his undivided attention. This was a special, quality time we spent together.

It was during this time that Dad taught me lessons about life. One of the most memorable was that I could do anything I wanted to do as long as I had a plan that was well-thought out. Sometimes, he would have me write my plan on the chalkboard in his room so that I could see it and make changes I needed.

1980s

IN DOROTHY'S WORDS:

Melissa was in college at Pittsburg when she and her high school sweetheart, Trent, announced they were going to have a baby. We had always liked Trent. They planned to get married, had sent out invitations, and all. Then two weeks before the wedding, it all fell apart.

Trent said, "I can't handle being a father or a husband."

"What is Melissa supposed to do?" I asked. I knew that his own father had been killed in a motorcycle accident just before his birth—was that part of the reason?

When Melissa was in labor, I didn't bother to call Trent. We helped Melissa with her baby, Zach, as she finished college.

A letter from Manuel, 1-26-90

Melissa,

Once again I want you to know I love you and Zachary. When Trent left you, I was hurt only because you were hurt. Yet in no way could I know your hurt.

In a situation like this as parents, we are only an audience. We cannot judge and dictate or in any way interfere with your life. However, you will know our concern as we offer our assistance. I'm happy that you allowed Zach to live with us.

The dialogue that follows places you and me on a defensive mood. Because we elected to raise you, naturally that causes us to vent our feeling. To our chagrin, nothing is accomplished.

Whatever you've decided to be or to do—we can only wish you success.

Basically, my sincere love for you stems from your understanding of me. Your love cards have always indicated as much. Thanks. You'll never know my deep feelings for you.

I would like also to include all my children. Each one of you is very special. I love you for what you are. Each of you are so different, but you've shown me personally that you care. Thanks.

Dad

1980s
IN DOROTHY'S WORDS:

Growing up, Melissa had always been curious about her past. We felt that was normal to wonder. We always said she was born to a king, because she liked fine things.

When she was 21-years-old, Melissa got her birth certificate. Through it, she found her biological mother's father. Her grandpa was shocked—he didn't even know she existed! Her mother, Marie-Claire, had been in college and not come home for Christmas before giving birth in January of 1966. Melissa found out that her mother was the youngest of thirteen children, all of whom had graduated college.

Her grandpa gave Melissa her mother's phone number. Then he sent her a check, saying it was for all the ice cream cones he had never given her as a little girl.

Melissa found out her mother lived in California and had earned five college degrees. Melissa called her around Easter time.

For a couple hours on the phone, Marie-Claire refused to acknowledge she'd had a baby. Then she 'fessed up. She invited Melissa, eighteen-month-old Zach and all of us to their family reunion in June.

THREE GENERATIONS OF PITTSBURG STATE GRADUATES:
MANUEL, MELISSA AND ZACHARY.

After meeting her daughter, Marie-Claire said, "I still know that I didn't make a mistake giving you up. College was more important."

Melissa replied, "I am in college and already have a baby. I will finish my degree but I would never give up my baby." It always saddens me how some difficulties show up in the next generation—we saw this with various children. However, sometimes a strong one breaks that vicious circle, like Melissa choosing differently than her mother. Marie-Claire is not a part of Melissa's life now.

It was different when she located her biological father, Mitch. He said he'd always wondered where his baby had gone. It was a wonderful experience.

Melissa met Greg at Pittsburg College when he was going to college and playing basketball. When they got married, both her biological dad, Mitch, and Manuel walked her down the aisle. Mitch always said he was so glad we shared her with him, and he treats her kids as his grandkids. Melissa and Greg had beautiful twins, Jade and Jordan.

After years of marriage, Melissa and Greg divorced. Their divorce finalized the weekend of Manuel's funeral. Melissa got the house. She wanted to move to Overland Park and put the house in Parsons on the market. It sat there for six months; then Greg bought it from her and moved back into my neighborhood.

"My kids grew up in this house," he told me. "If you need me at all, I'd be happy to help." He always was a kind guy.

I know Melissa will always care for him as the father of her children. It's better to be nice to each other than bitter, I think.

Melissa's biological father Mitch also came from Chicago for Manuel's funeral, and for other events, like in 2014 for the graduations of Melissa's twins—from Kansas University and Friends University. Melissa had a wonderful celebration for them. Jade's graduation was May 18, on Manuel's birthday, and Jordan's May 10. Manuel would have been so proud.

After Manuel died, Melissa married Gary in Florida in 2012. Mitch walked her down the aisle. She had sand dollars inscribed with some of Manuel's prayers.

God, You are a loving, sustaining and supportive presence in my life. Be with me always, especially when doubts cross my attention. Amen.

Our dear daughter has certainly gone through tribulations. She has grown into a compassionate woman and is a social worker. She worked for Harry Hynes Hospice. I know some of our caring for children rubbed off onto our daughters.

Melissa has raised a foster son, Zach, with many special needs issues. He went to school at the State Hospital and is now twenty-one-years-old. She has done a beautiful job with him. He even has a job as a cart-pusher at Wal-Mart now. I am so proud of him.

RITA:

RITA'S SENIOR PICTURE 1985.

We adopted Rita as a baby when Melissa was about eighteen-months-old. Rita was an easy-going child. I never made Rita dresses like I had for her sister—she was my tomboy. I was worried about people comparing them. They were different, like apples and oranges. That didn't stop them from being close growing up.

They played on the same basketball team. I remember a big game that was tied and Rita scored from half-court!

Rita does a wonderful job at the state hospital. I get compliments on her caring ways from people. She'll work double shifts and then be on call at the Youth Crisis Center. She's also a certified referee for various sports throughout the year.

When the girls were twenty-one-years-old, they got their original birth certificates. We knew Rita had come from Garden City, and her name was listed as Baby Girl Rojas.

It was when Melissa was working at the hospital in Parsons that Rita met a connection to her past. Melissa was enrolling new clients and a couple brought in a young boy with mental problems. They were from Garden City, with the last name Rojas. Melissa thought the father looked like he could be Rita's brother.

Melissa called Rita and asked if she wanted her to ask if they could be related. Rita said yes.

It turned out to be Rita's cousin. Through them, she met her grandparents from Wichita, who were sweet people. She found out her biological father's name was Manuel, and her mother's name was Suzie—we had named her Rita Suzanne without knowing this.

Rita was the third child of a nineteen-year-old girl. Rita's father didn't marry her mother, but instead married her mother's sister and had five more kids. Rita didn't feel she needed to meet a man who hadn't treated her mother right.

However, he was at Rita's grandpa's funeral, shaking hands with people in the receiving line. It was an uncomfortable situation. Afterward, I asked Rita if she had met and talked with her biological father.

"I just shook his hand, that's all, Mom," she said.

Yes, it's a different world with adoption. But I've always been grateful to the girls' biological parents that they made daughters for us.

IN RITA'S WORDS:

My dad is and always will be my hero. He supported me and my sister in all our sports and was at every game. He always said, "I got my girls who play sports and my boys who play piano. That's what makes my life special—my kids!"

Letter from Manuel to all his children:

"I wish I could hold you more."
Under this canopy of blue – we are together – however the distance that may be. Each in your own lifestyle has given joy to the fullest measure. I love you. Thanks!

IN 1980 FOUR BIOLOGICAL SONS AND TWO ADOPTED DAUGHTERS
BACK LEFT: BRIAN, RON, DANIEL,
FRONT LEFT: MARTIN, MELISSA, RITA.

1980s
IN DOROTHY'S WORDS :
RONALD:

I went to the hospital with Melissa for the birth of her son, Zach. When I got home, I found that Manuel had accepted an eight-year-old foster boy, Ronald. That made me a new grandmother and a new mother all on the same day!

Ronald's mother had been a student in Manuel's classroom in high school. By the time she finished high school, she had Ronald and his little sister, Cassidy, who were taken from her. They were split up and put in different foster homes—something I still don't understand or agree with from the system! Their mom moved to California after school and had five more children.

Unfortunately, Ronald's first foster home wasn't a good situation. It was pathetic really. He was taken out of that home and brought to us. We would've taken both him and his sister, but that didn't happen.

He was an easy child to raise and became one of us. We adopted him when he was twelve-years-old.

RONALD'S SENIOR PICTURE IN 1995

When he was a senior, Ronald got in with the wrong crowd and got in trouble. He was in Missouri with a friend in a car the friend had stolen. When they were picked up, Ronald got in trouble too and was held in the jail in Carthage.

Letter from Ronald in 1997—Manuel's written responses in parentheses

Dad,

Hello. How's my dad doing these days (I've often thought of you). Me, not too good because I'm sitting in "Jasper County Jail" for a crime I didn't even do. But plus I was thinking about how wrong I've been toward you.

And I was just wondering if you could give me another chance to prove to you that I can be just like the rest of your sons. Because sometimes I stay up late crying because I really messed up because you don't even want me as your son anymore because I've done all this stuff that Martin, Daniel, Brian, Ron (come visit with them—I'm sure you'd be surprised) didn't do when they was young and about my age.

I know they had a job at that age. Plus they got up every morning and went to work with you. So I just thought I would write you this letter. Because when I come back I would like us to start all over again if we can. Plus I want to go to work with you.

It's just when you yell at me it makes me kinda scared that's all and you're probably wondering why I'm just now telling you this. Because you don't give me a chance to ask or say anything. (Come and share time with us. We have been concerned about you.)

Yes, I want to make you and Mom proud of me. It's just that you have to go slow with me. So I want to know if it's ok for me to come back home and be with my family. (You have the name. You have always been welcomed.) That's if you guys still want me as your son. But this time I'm asking you this, not Mom, not Rita, not anybody but you. (As my son, I'm sorry you did not realize my concern for your future.)

And me and Jason was going to rent that house of yours. Like I said, I want to make you proud just like the rest of your sons did. But you just have to give me more time. And I want you in my life until the day I die. Plus when I die you will still be in there. I want us to be very close to each other. Can we do that? (You belong here.) I wasn't going to come back until you read this letter, but I guess I will give it to you face to face.

So like I say I'm so sorry for being like that towards you. I want us to be able to sit down together, and sit back and talk. I want you to come over and sit and visit with me and I want to be able to do the same thing. Plus I want to know if I have something on my mind that I can come to you and we sit down and talk about it like grown men do. (I'll never know until you ask.)

That's all that I want to be able to do. I would like it if you could be kinda like my best friend. But when I go to work with you we can like be able to work together and you can teach me all the stuff that you know.

All I want is a dad to love me (come home and be part of the family) and who is willing to take the time to kick it with his son. I just miss my family so much.

And I know that I've never told you before but Dad, I really miss you a lot. I've always wanted to be like you but I couldn't so I just did all of this stuff. Sometimes I just don't know why you and Mom wasted your time on me to be your son when you have five already.

I know I could never really be a real Perez like the other boys are. So I just think that if you don't want to take the time to teach me, then I guess I should leave the Perez family forever (Never.) Right?

I just want you to love me, Dad. Well, I guess I will go now, but thanks for everything that you have done for me. Bye, love yah, Dad.

Love, your stepchild Ronald Ray Martin (I don't think I'm good enough to wear the last name Perez)

IN DOROTHY'S WORDS :

Ronald dated Stacy in high school. I was close friends with her mom, Sherry. Ronald and Stacy had two children, and then he left. I felt it was another sad recycling of what his own mother had done with her family.

Stacy takes good care of the kids, with the help of her mom. She works in the kitchen at the hospital here. The children, Jevan and Jasmine, are sweet kids and both athletes. The Jasmine is on the boys' football team and I love watching her.

Ronald moved to Pittsburg and has two more children.

Of course, with Ron Perez and Ronald Perez, there's been some administration confusion with bank accounts and once with a driver's license. Ron is a truck driver and was up in the north when he was stopped by a state trooper.

"You're driving on a suspended license!" said the trooper.

"Oh, blame my mom," said Ron.

The trooper was confused. "What does your mom have to do with this?"

"See, my mom is always dragging in all these kids. That's my kid brother, Ronald!" Ron was saved by his middle initial, as sixteen-year-old Ronald did indeed have a suspended license. We call them Ron and Ronald to keep them separate.

CHAPTER ELEVEN

You Know You're
Foster Parent When...

IN DOROTHY'S WORDS, ADAPTED FROM OTHER LISTS:
The nurse at the doctor's office smiles, welcomes you by your first name and then goes on a three-hour coffee break.

You have a dark-haired six-month-old and a blonde, blue-eyed three-month-old in a double stroller and people constantly stop you and ask, "Are they twins?"

You go to the park with just your family and have enough people for a football game.

Strangers approach you in the mall and ask, "Don't you know where babies come from?"

Your personal stash of children's clothing rivals that of the local Goodwill store. (I thought of this when I came across two bags, one full of socks and the other full of mittens. The 25 cent price tags were still on each item. I always bought things on sale. Now I give them to my great-grandchildren and hope they will like the style.)

Someone says to you, "Do you know what Johnny did today?" and you reply, "Go ahead, surprise me and make my day!"

You have two dark-haired boys both named Ronald. They have the same last name of Perez. The first is a biological son, the second an adopted son.

The owner of the local grocery store knows you by your name.

School returns to session after a vacation and you constantly sing, "It's the most wonderful time of the year!"

Your case worker asks you to take a child for just a few days, and you know what that <u>really</u> means.

The phrase "basically a good child with a few problems" doesn't mean the same thing coming from a case worker as it does in the real world.

Saying goodnight resembles the end of The Waltons— "Goodnight, Jon Boy." "Good night, Mary Ellen."

Bedtimes are split into every half hour, and there seems to be an age appropriate kid for each time.

You eat in shifts, and you can't remember if you ate.

When your head hits the pillow at night, you giggle. Another thing, instead of counting sheep, you count kids jumping a fence to go to sleep.

Light switches, toilet handles and door knobs last one year or less.

The fella at the shoe store knows your first name. (When I first brought Minoru, the salesmen asked what shoe size. He about fell off the stool when Minoru said size 25!)

You are one of the few people who purchase the extended warranty on a washing machine, while smiling at the nice sales-man who thinks he's getting one over on you. (I always wanted to take a picture of my big family standing by my washing machine and send it to the Maytag Company.)

The family wears the same color of t-shirt when you go places so you can always find them. (When we went to Disney World the first time, I actually made each of us a striped top and embroidered their initials on each shirt pocket.)

Parent/teacher meeting nights are "a night out."

People constantly tell you that they "couldn't" give up the kids like you do. (This was always the hardest part about foster parenting.)

You need $50 or more just to go to McDonalds.

Your idea of a "social life" is talking to the cashiers at the grocery store.

You have been changing diapers for more years than you can remember, with no end in sight.

Your children's teacher has your number on speed dial. (It was with our last foster boy, Johnny, that we bought our first cellphone, as his school was always trying to get ahold of us.)

The principal of the public school locks his door when he sees you coming.

FYI, by Jim Davis, Parsons Sun

Jim Davis would call me all the time to find out "how the world turns." Here's a story I sent him in 1966.

We hate to mention our names as we do many zany things all the time, and we do not want the publicity. Both my friend and I live on the west side of town and in our two households there is a combined figure of thirteen children. So we do not have time to visit with each other during the day.

We each have a plug-in phone and have long extension chords for them. After we get all the kids down for the night, we usually call each other for our evening chat.

The other night I took my phone to bed to do my chatting. My husband was already asleep and snoring. As my friend and I rambled from one topic to another, I dozed off...leaving her in a terrible predicament.

She and her husband took turns listening to me snore. They thought about driving out to hang up the phone, but they figured the door would be locked.

Then they decided to hang up their phone, knowing the beeper would come on my phone. It did, and I shot out of bed frightening my husband. But it did wake me up.

The next day my friend's husband said it proved two points—we are dull conversationalists and we never really have anything of importance to say. Now when he sees me, he starts singing "Sleepytime Gal."

Letter by Dorothy to Social and Rehabilitation Services in the early 1970s

Dear Helen and all with whom we have been connected in the offices,

It is late this evening and <u>they</u> are all asleep! I have these feelings often but I felt like writing about them this time.

First of all, I have thanked God for all my own brown-eyed, tan-skinned children. Then I guess I must thank each of you for considering us for the rest of <u>our</u> children with whom we have been blessed. Yes, they have each been a blessing in a different way and when the whole group has been joined as a family unit, our whole life has been a wonderful experience.

You will never know how great it is to walk out the front door, looking like a typical "scrub woman," with the kids all waiting in our van to go the store. As you approach the van, they all shout in unison, "Yay, Mom, yay!" I have a real cheering section!

We feel bad the way it has turned out with Bobby Nelson. He is a sweet guy. We only hope his stay in Salina will be the best thing for his future.

Then there is his sister Joan. She has been my calendar keeper—she remembers every appointment we have. In fact, whe seems to know what step I'm going to take next. She has been such a helper through the years. She's swell.

We learned a whole new language when the Nelson children moved in. Manuel and I say to each other that we know Spanish, English and the Nelson language. It is a special language which we will always treasure. Our kitchen will always be the "kitching" to Joan and we still use that word. However, we used to go to the "Munexican building" for programs and now we just go to the <u>Municipal</u> building.

We are proud of Roland, who was a straight F student and was difficult to live with. Manuel kept saying to me, "We aren't mad at Roland—we are mad at his past." Well, Roland made the honor roll these last nine weeks. He isn't with us now, but we are proud of him. He came Saturday evening for a birthday supper and Bobby's going away party. Roland told me he was glad we stood by him when we did.

I was rocking Harold the other afternoon and the thought of his and his brother Teddy's departure day hit me and the tears started flowing. Of course he didn't know why I cried. But we know that a mom and dad somewhere are waiting for these special little guys and we will be so happy for them.

Now we have a new member. We don't know Carol too well, but we'll try our best. It is important to us that she will soon be laughing all the time.

I've got to thank the Perez kids. I believe they have learned compassion. Maybe some days they have been in the background when we have had to spend extra time on kids who didn't have too good of a beginning.

Then there is Manuel. Without him, it couldn't be done. He is our organizer. I can cook and wash all day, but things wouldn't go right at all if he didn't have the know-how for herding, loving, disciplining and teaching.

There have been sad days, but we try to think of the fun days. Like Teddy—he can't seem to ever find his coat or one of his shoes. For two days this week, we couldn't find his coat and he had to wear Rita's. Had I only dusted under his bed sooner like I should, he wouldn't have had to wear a flowered coat to kindergarten. Guess it didn't matter much what the teacher thought about the coat, because I discovered Rita was wearing Teddy's train engineer boots to school. She made me promise to buy her some. She's our tom-boy. Guess I should pin notes on the so the teacher will understand and won't think I send them off to school this way.

Oh, the funny stories we have. The other day, I looked outside the window to check on little Harold. To my dismay, he did not have a stitch of clothes on and was very busy taking a bath in a mud puddle!

We have our first wedding this month, our first born Danny, which means we will gain another family member. I know I should be sewing dresses for all the girl family members right now. But I felt like writing and I do best at getting things done at the last moment anyway. Danny is trying to use as many of the children in the wedding as possible and we are all getting so excited.

Manuel sometimes tells people he goes from one classroom situation in the daytime to another classroom situation at night. He has also told people it would be nice to maybe come home to a quiet evening of newspaper or TV. But he says after all, we don't get to do this and there must be a reason—we love kids!

Some people need sleeping pills at night. Some people don't know what to do with their time. But as I crawl into bed each night, I can't help thinking of what a great, busy day it was...and I'm asleep!

Thanks for all you have done for us. We love your kids and our door will always be open to them. I'm thankful to have had the opportunity to receive children three different ways—natural, foster and adoption.

Sincerely,
Dorothy Perez

CHAPTER TWELVE

Many More Mini Stories

Usually, our foster kids were from poor or broken homes. Once Rita came running down the stairs and said, "Did we get a new kid in the middle of the night?"

"No," I said confused.

"Well, there's a kid in pajamas in my room, playing with the TV," she said. He had escaped from the state hospital and had just come right in the door.

A friend mentioned on a visit, that I always used to get all the flowers on Mother's Day in church, when they gave a flower for each child. I didn't always feel like going because of that. There were other large families, but I always won!

Once a social worker found a mother who had been living out of her car. She was just handing out her kids to whoever would take them.

Late 1980s-1990s

We had three little brothers who came to us. Their parents were doing horrible things to the kids and were in prison in Topeka.

We enjoyed having the boys with us. Spencer was the oldest, then Joe and Jerry. I think Jerry was about eight or nine-years-old when they arrived, and they stayed with us through high school.

Jerry had made a close friend out of our neighbor's boy. They were a nice family, and when they moved across town, Jerry went to stay one night.

The boys went out to ride their bikes. They shouldn't have but they went to the creek. It had been a bad rainy season, and the creek was dangerously flooded. Jerry's friend drowned. They searched all night for his body.

It was an accident. But it was a shock to the whole town. The boy's mother gave a nice talk at the middle school assembly that year and donated a tree in his memory that is still growing there. Jerry struggled with the loss.

We came across a note from the principal at the school about Jerry. I don't recall anything about the incident, but apparently he was suspended for four days. "This action is being taken due to Jerry's continuing problem of breaking rules. On this particular occasion, Jerry's poor judgement resulted in an injury to another student. The student was taken for medical treatment with a possible punctured eardrum."

The boys had problems related to their parents—they had grown up in such a bad situation. And I feel poor Jerry who was deeply affected by the drowning accident.

His older brother Spencer called me recently. I've meant to call Jerry. It sounds like even his brother has lost touch with him.

One boy was from Honduras. The authorities found him in a railroad box car, and he only spoke Spanish. They contacted us, because they knew Manuel could communicate with him. He only stayed for one night, but it wasn't the only time that Manuel helped the police with translation. (Now our sweet Mexican daughter-in-law Sonia volunteers and does translation, even going to the hospital with a mother in labor.)

~⁀○

1970s

One year, we had four kids in kindergarten—Rita, Teddy, Agnes and Roxie. Agnes and Roxie were sisters. They weren't twins, but close enough in age to both be in kindergarten. Two kids went in the morning, and the other two went in the afternoon.

One morning, the principal called. "Dorothy, you dropped off the wrong two and someone else was in their seat. You have upset the whole school system!"

We got Agnes and Roxie because we already had their big sister, Carol. When she arrived, Carol was deathly sick. I had never seen such diarrhea. She was pale, and I knew she needed immediate help.

I took her to the doctor, but it was a new one who didn't know us. She took a quick look at Carol and said accusingly, "You have not been feeding this child!"

"I haven't gotten the chance to—she's new," I said, explaining that we were her foster parents.

"I'm not even going to examine her. Take her to the hospital right away," said the doctor.

However, here we hit a bureaucratic snag. "They won't treat Carol without a parent's signature!" I told the social worker desperately. As a foster parent, I could take her to the hospital but couldn't sign for her.

The whole point of the girls being in our county was to hide their whereabouts from their psychotic parents. They had come to protest and had thrown mud on the welfare building. However, the social worker had to call and get the father's signature for Carol. That of course gave away the hospital and then the location of our house.

After a while, they allowed the girls to visit their parents on weekends. I would pack their suitcases full of clean clothes. When they came back one Sunday night with only dirty clothes, little Roxie said with a lisp, "Daddy says you can wash our dirty clothes 'cause he doesn't like Japanese, and he doesn't like Mexicans." This was in the early 1970s, when Minoru was with us.

The girls stayed with us through high school. Later, Carol lived in Chanute. We were there one September for the Mexican Fiesta, just sitting on the bleachers. Someone poked me in the rear—I turned around and there was Carol. We were so glad to see her.

After she was married, one day we had a knock on the door. Carol said, "I wanted my son to see where I grew up."

⁓⊘

In the summer, the social worker called me and asked if she could bring a child. I had an appointment, but my son Ron was able to watch them until I got back.

When I arrived, the kids were in a circle in the yard, just laughing. Ron said, "Mom, you're gonna like this one."

"Well, I think I like all of them," I said.

"He's going to be our entertainer."

The boy had a cleft palate, and he was drinking and then shooting water up through his nose!

⁓⊘

2006

In our last family portrait, we had a surprising addition. One of our renters hosted a foreign exchange student. "I don't know how to entertain him," she told me.

"We are doing family pictures, and then I am making a Mexican dinner," I said. "If he'd like, he can join us for the dinner."

The student arrived before we were through with pictures. Later, my daughter-in-law pointed to the swarm of faces in the portrait. "Who is that guy?"

The student had automatically gotten in our picture too. We had never seen him before or since, but he'll always be in our family picture. He enjoyed our Mexican food too.

OUR CHILDREN AND GRANDCHILDREN. THE EXCHANGE STUDENT IS THE DARK-HAIRED YOUNG MAN IN THE FAR LEFT.

1950s

My brother, John, and his wife, Norma, couldn't have children. So in 1959, they adopted little Carol Anne from a college girl.

One day, John called me. "You wouldn't have a couple of extra beds available to borrow now, would you?"

"Well, they're all full right now. Why?" I asked.

"We're going to get four kids today," he said. They were foster kids. The oldest, Glenda, was four-years-old, down to a baby. Glenda would pull up a chair and do dishes, because she felt her responsibility to her younger siblings so strongly. With baby Carol Anne, they had five kids under the age of four. John and Norma were willing, and even thrilled to pieces. But it was a little overwhelming.

Then John had an idea. Their close friends, Charlie and Rosie, who owned the Ace Hardware in town, couldn't have children either. John asked if they could take the two younger children. The state approved this plan. All four children grew up together, going to the same schools, church and such. Twelve years after the adoptions, Norma suddenly became pregnant and had a daughter, Kim.

When the children were grown, Glenda was married and had a six-week-old baby, Kerri. In a horrible accident, Glenda was electrocuted and died. Her husband survived, but wasn't well. John and Norma adopted in the baby. Glenda's brother Alan calls Kerri his niecester—by blood his niece and by adoptiong his sister. Our curly-headed Bliss used to touch Keri's red curls admiringly. Kerri now teaches special education.

My brother John had been a farmer and an insurance adjuster, busy with travel. When he was older, he lost his business in the Parsons tornado and wasn't well. I don't know what was wrong, but he just gave up and sat in his chair. Norma took good care of him.

One day, Norma was out mowing the yard and was stung by a bee. Her reaction was serious enough to put her in the hospital. They dismissed her the next day, as she seemed fine. However, two days later, she passed away suddenly.

That was hard on John. He lived in a nursing home for four months before he joined Norma. He kept thinking the nursing home was one of the hotels he stayed at when he was away on business.

I visited him there one day and showed him my girlhood diary. As kids, we got a quarter as an allowance per month and Dad would buy us a sack of candy. He divided it up between the three of us. I always hoarded mine to make it last, but the boys would steal it from me. In my diary, I wrote, "John owes me five cents."

At the nursing home, I said, "John, you are really indebted to me. You owe me five cents."

"I hope I don't owe you interest," John replied.

2015

In sharing the episodes of our family and our lifestyle, you can see how Manuel's love of education has trickled on down to our children and grandchildren.

In May, we have a granddaughter, Selena and a great-grand-daughter, Kiersten, graduating together from Labette County High School and then they will be off to college in the fall.

Our graduates from college include:

Melissa – Pittsburg State University

Zachary – Pittsburg State University

Jade – University of Kansas

Jordan – Friends University

Lisa – Pittsburg State University (she is now a teacher)

Sara – Pittsburg State University

Jeremiah – University of Kansas

Rachele – Pittsburg State University (She attached Manuel's picture to her graduation gown because she wanted Grandpa to walk with her.)

Lauren – Kansas State University

CHAPTER THIRTEEN

The Blind Musician

1980s

IN DOROTHY'S WORDS :

I got a call from the Parsons' school district, asking me if I would serve as a blind boy's paraprofessional at the middle school. I wasn't looking for work. It was 1981 and I had eleven kids at home, including foster children. They said they really wanted me, though.

The school wanted me to work with Jack, who was born blind and needed a one-on-one aid.

Since it was a school position and I would be home when the children were, I thought it would work. It was a wonderful experience for me.

We went everywhere together. I even went to the boy's gym class and we ran laps and did what the other boys did.

It was rewarding—not monetarily, but rewarding. It was fascinating what we did. I started with him in middle school and then went on with him through high school. I would read his lessons as needed—he would do his math on an abacus!

Jack learned to play music by ear at a young age. He didn't read sheet music. He said he didn't believe in it. "They have

Braille music, but who has time for that?" he said. He studied under music teacher Jim Kindall and Dana Saliba.

Once, while he was in middle school, I took him to the Special Olympics for the Performing Arts in Salina. The cleaners here loaned us a tux, and we got a candelabra to set on the piano. He was very independent. They introduced him with all the other kids, but he had to go up and introduce himself.

I was with Jack for three years at the middle school and then in high school, he was in Manuel's special ed class. They asked if I could let Manuel be my boss.

I replied, with a laugh, "I'll let him be the boss at school but I'll be the boss when we get home."

Jack was the first blind student to graduate from PHS. He attempted going to college to study music, but "music is the only thing I ever got A's in," he said.

Blindness Helps Jack Develop Ear For Music
PARSONS SUN
by Julie Mah, January 28, 1984

Darkness. To live your life knowing everyone around you can see, except you. Jack knows that feeling every day he goes to school.

Jack, a sophomore at Parsons High School, has been blind from birth. He has hypoplasia of the optic lobe, which means the optic nerves never develop. He lives with his mother, Carol, and younger brother, Frank.

This year is his third year in the Parsons public school system, after attending the Kansas School for the Blind in Kansas City, Kan., for eight years.

He says it only took him three days to master the layout of the high school building. He uses a white cane, which he has used for two years, to go from class to class.

He is in the special education program at the high school and also attends other classes in the building.

"He is actually his own teacher," said Dorothy Perez, a paraprofessional who works with Jack in the special education classes and accompanies him to his classes.

Mrs. Perez dictates lessons to Jack and helps him throughout the day with his homework, but sometimes he doesn't need her guidance.

"When we show films in class," she said, "Jack picks up more than other kids who can see. His memory is better. He is a very special person."

His ability to remember things has translated into a growing love for music. He has two classes in music. He also plays the piano, sings in choir and is in the Music Co., a group that performs for school assemblies and activities.

"I like them (the music classes)," the 15 year-old said. "I could go to them 24 hours a day. I'm hooked on that. It's just like math, it's one note plus another."

Although he has never learned to "read" music, Jack is able to hear a song and reproduce it on the piano, with his own revisions to the song.

"It's better to improvise than to follow along," he said. "It's hard to follow along."

He hopes to use his musical talent when he is ready to find a job.

I'd like to talk somebody into making records," he said. "Or maybe be a disc jockey." A teenage deejay is something Jack thinks is needed in the area.

"I don't see why KLKC or any other radio station can't let me do it (deejay), just once."

Jack doesn't consider being blind a handicap, but he says he sometimes wonders what it would be like to see.

"I'm used to being blind, I kind of like it," he said. "But in some ways I wish I could see. But then I would have to go back to school to learn to read and write."

When Jack turns 16 on May 1, he will be able to work or continue his education. He says he hasn't really planned his future.

"I don't know what I want," he said. "I'd like to make some money. I want to get out there. I want to be a free man, act like all the sighted people."

Performer Moves Back to Town
Portions taken from a 2013 Parsons Sun article by Colleen Surridge

"I did not do well academically. I used to take IQ tests they would give me and I didn't pass anything well. They said I had the equivalent of about an eighth-grade education," Jack said. "I was not textbook smart. The psychologists and psychometrists told me assembly line work was about all I could ever do, and that was questionable. I was in special education most of my childhood. I had a slight learning disability, and I would have to hear something two or three times, or have someone like take my hand and walk me through it, or show me how to understand."

What he did know was he could play the piano and he loved to sing. Moving to Missouri, he got with his first band.

"I played in bands in honky tonks. I was in and out of bands over the years because of musicians that couldn't cut it or I couldn't cut it in their opinion. I've been a one-man band, and been in two-man bands, three and four-man bands," he said. "I've played for private parties and events, weddings and county fairs. One time,

I opened for Ronnie McDowell. He put on a fantastic show. He's a heck of an entertainer."

Bands often found themselves short a bass player, so Buskirk learned how to play bass on his keyboard with his left hand while playing piano chords with his right.

His preference for music falls into the categories of old country and classic rock. "I like musicians like Conway Twitty, Merle Haggard, Eddie Arnold, Hank Williams, Red Foley, and I like classic rock like Foghat, AC/DC and Van Halen," he said.

Music outside the realm of his preference, he doesn't perform, he said, "because it's not my style...I hate disco, rap and hip-hop."

One of his most recent continual gigs was playing in Branson at a steak house.

"When he would play in Branson, he would let me know. I've gone to watch him a couple of times," said Dorothy Perez. "It's fun now because the kids I took care of are part of me. It makes life interesting."

Tired of living in the city and longing to return home closer to friends and family, Buskirk contacted Perez to see if she would help he and his wife, Donna, relocate back to Parsons. Perez graciously opened her home to her former student until he and his wife could find a place of their own.

"I turned to Dorothy because she is a friend of mine that I've come to respect a lot. I've been waiting to move back down here where you can enjoy life, keep it simple and keep it slow," he said.

Now settled into a place of their own, Buskirk said he would like to find some gigs, local events, nightclubs or special occasions to play.

"I like doing what I do," he said. "It's that or making fries or sacking groceries...and walking the groceries out to the car is where I draw the line."

As for costs for him to perform, he said he charges $25 an hour if he is performing a one-man show. Also, because he cannot drive and has no car, he usually will require transportation to the event and home.

"It's just hobby pay that helps cover the cost of wear and tear on my equipment and lets me have a little extra money for bills," he said. "If people want to see me play, I used to play with the Honkey Tonk Blues band; I played for Jeff Ward and played with Rod Hizey and Jim Robinson, a very good friend of mine. I was in the band Close Enough For Country with Brian Dering."

"I remember my first gig was for Sam Lenati. I played for his little boy John. He played sax. I played and earned 25 bucks. That was big money. Then I got scheduled after school to go to KLKC and I did a commercial for Talking Books under Martin Kinzie. The next thing I know, I was at my breakfast nook, eating breakfast and was hearing the commercial and my own voice coming over the radio. I didn't get paid, but I was a celeb for a couple of months. I would be walking down the halls at school and people would stop and tell me, 'I heard you on the radio.' That was a long time ago. I've played out now for 25 years, and that's what I'd like to keep doing."

IN DOROTHY'S WORDS:

I called and talked to Jack recently. He said it was lucky I had caught him as he is playing with a traveling band going to Texas. I had hoped after the Sun article that he would get more music jobs in Parsons. I'm so proud; he's such a good pianist.

CHAPTER FOURTEEN
There's No Place Like Home

1950s-1960s
IN DOROTHY'S WORDS :

THE HOUSE AS IT IS TODAY.

When Manuel and I bought our house, it wasn't really a very good house. It just had four little rooms. But we were happy with it, and our payment was only $50 per month. And as Dorothy says in the Wizard of Oz, there's no place like home.

After we had our first two boys, Manuel started adding on to the house. We had the piano from my childhood. As he worked,

Manuel would push the piano to the next room. Finally, he ended up shoving the piano into the bathroom through a closet wall.

When Manuel was ready to move the piano out, he got it through the door but couldn't turn it in the new hallway. So the piano stayed in the bathroom. For five years.

One Sunday afternoon, our friends Lee and Betty were over and their little girl, Kathy, asked me if she could go play the piano.

"I didn't know you guys had a piano," said Lee. I showed him.

As a newspaper photographer, he wanted to tell the paper about it. "It's too embarrassing!" I said. Finally, I said he could if he didn't use our names. Of course, he used them anyway. By Tuesday morning, everyone knew we had a piano in the bathroom.

Then it hit the Associated Press and was on television. That story just went on and on. We got letters from everyone with ideas and opinions. A nurse from the Washington D.C. area sent a letter saying we needed a registered piano technician to dismantle it. I thought that was funny. She obviously didn't know Parsons was a small town. There was even a carpenter who offered to come and get it out for us!

At the end of the year, the AP did a review of stories with bathrooms and included ours along with one about Marilyn Monroe's bathroom with mink walls.

Eventually, Manuel cut a hole in the wall to get the piano out.

As The Perez Family Grows So Does Their Casa
Parsons Sun, October 1969

Mr. and Mrs. Manuel Perez of Route 3 had an average-sized family: four.

Now their family has grown. There are eight children now. They increased their flock with two adopted children and two foster children.

The Perez' soon discovered that adopting children brought complications. Mainly the house.

State regulations on adoption are strict about housing. For example, the Perez' had to build a fire escape from their second story. And they also had to install fire extinguishers on both floors.

Then came the need for more space and as Perez is handy with tools, he set about increasing the size of the home. From a four-room abode it grew to a sprawling, Spanish-styled seven bedroom house. All the handiwork of Perez.

IN DOROTHY'S WORDS:

If our walls could talk! Our upstairs bedrooms actually do, with themes that tell our stories.

In one, we display things sent from our Japanese student's mother. Porcelain-faced dolls in red kimonos sit on a shiny black and gold dresser, ornate vases, fans and a box on the matching vanity. A watered silk dress, a gift from my Navy pilot brother, hangs next to the night stand and a tiny tea set.

Another bedroom, is my Pioneer Room. I have my parents' walnut bed and the signed picture of Will Rogers from when Dad met him. There are old photographs of me as a baby, and mom in a stair-step line with her five sisters, including the adopted oldest sister.

I also started a year-round Christmas-themed room upstairs. I wanted to have a tree decorated, a miniature train going around it and a rocking chair, where I could sit and watch the grandkids play. I do have some decorations up there, but I never did finish it.

Downstairs, I have an Africa-themed room, dedicated to our African-American children with their photographs. There are wall hangings and a straw monkey that Ron brought home from his fourth-grade trip to Chicago. I also have a gorgeous African angel.

I always wanted to have a bed and breakfast, with folks staying in the different themed rooms. But at eighty-six-years-old, it's not going to happen now!

Of course, my biggest theme is the Wizard of Oz. I have memorabilia items scattered over the house. In the garden, I have wooden statues of the Lion, the Tinman and the Scarecrow, carved from logs by a chainsaw artist.

Dorothy Has Her Own Yellow Brick Road
by Colleen Surridge
Parsons Sun, May 11, 2011

While some natives of Kansas tire of people of other states connecting them with the Land of Oz, the association is one native Kansan Dorothy Perez willingly adopted early in life.

"Being born in Kansas and having the first name Dorothy, it has always kind of been my theme," said Perez.

The association with the famous 1939 film, "The Wizard of Oz," became even more pronounced when Perez was swept into a "different world" complete with munchkins—dozens and dozens of munchkins.

Mrs. Perez married in December 1950 to her husband, Manuel Perez, and six months later, he purchased more than 2.5 acres, containing a small house, appropriately situated on Dorothy Street.

"It was just a shack, built out of ammunition boxes, and Manuel built it into this," she said, showing pictures of the original shack beside pictures of it expanded to a seven bedroom home.

The expansion was necessary, as since early childhood, she dreamed of having at least a dozen children...

Oftentimes the couple would have more children than their foster license permitted, but Perez said the state was the one violating the number of children allowed. They simply opened their arms and accepted the children...

Some children remained with the Perez family from early childhood to adulthood, others stayed a few months or years and were gone.

"I never did reach a dozen kids. The most I ever had at a time was 11," she said.

"We had children in our home for 45 years. Altogether, we had 94 foster children that were long-term. That number doesn't include the overnighters," she said. "It's been wonderful, but there have been many tears, too."

It also doesn't include the number of older youths and young adults the couple brought into their home through foreign exchange programs.

"I always called us the Neopolitan family, because we came in all shades," she said.

The couple were honored in Topeka for their 45 years of service to the Kansas Children's Service League, but one of the greatest tributes to the couple's work can be found in their own backyard.

Mr. Perez decided he would build a "yellow brick road" in his wife's garden, with bricks marking the family's history.

The path begins with the names of the couple's parents, then moves on to include them and their natural born children and then many of their long-term foster children and even some of their exchange students.

While her husband is now passed, Mrs. Perez said her children continue to help her add bricks to the path. Many of her foster children come to visit her still, and seeing the path, wish to be added as one of her children.

Even Minoru, her Japanese foreign exchange student for two years, expressed his desire to have he and his wife and children's names added as part of the family.

Looking out across the path, surrounded by every color of iris, Perez said, "It's been a wonderful experience..."

THE YELLOW BRICK ROAD.

2014

IN DOROTHY'S WORDS:

We are moving my yellow brick road to the eighty-five acres my brothers and I inherited from our parents. There's a lovely pond and a park shelter. We've had many picnics out there. It will be a good time to update and add names to my road.

Parsons Sun
F.Y.I. by Jim Davis, November 1975

Don't go up on the front porch at 513 N. 32nd and knock on the front door. The door knob doesn't work. As a matter of fact, neither does the door because the door isn't really a door.

What appears to be a door is only a picture painted by Arlita McClure, art instructor for Parsons elementary schools.

Why the illusion? Well, it was the idea of Dorothy Perez. Mrs. Perez and her husband, Manuel C. Perez, special education teacher in Parsons schools, own the little olive and black colored house. The Perezes like to remodel houses. They live at the northwest corner of the city on a street named Dorothy (after Mrs. Perez) in a house they remodeled in the Spanish motif.

Long ago, while they were remodeling their own home, they accidentally built a piano into a bathroom. FYI blabbed about this so loudly that the story of the piano in the bathroom got around all over the country. After a year or so, the Perezes got tired of hearing about it and we promised to quit bringing up the subject.

But that has nothing to do with the phony front door at 513. They closed a door on the west end, facing 32nd, and put it on the north side of the house.

This left the front porch without a door, which is a rather odd looking sight. So, reasoned Mrs. Perez, why not paint a false door on the wall?

Arlita McClure was commissioned for the project. She was a natural choice. She lives near the Perezes in a mobile home. "I sew for her and she paints for me," said Mrs. Perez. "Arlita is figuring out something to paint on it."

Lest you think Dorothy Perez owns all the imagination in the family, consider what her husband concocted. He faced the problem of building a stone garage that would match the house the Perezes acquired on Pefly Street near where they live. When he could find no matching stone, he made some, following much experimentation, with cement. A friend suggested that in making rocks, Perez might be getting into divine territory.

CHAPTER FIFTEEN

We're Not in Kansas Anymore

1960s

IN DOROTHY'S WORDS :

The fact that Manuel taught school for thirty-seven years did allow us many long summer trips. I still love to travel. This Dorothy actually liked to pack up and say, "Toto, we're not in Kansas anymore!"

A very special trip was in 1967. Manuel had been chosen as one of thirty-six teachers from all over the USA to go to the Institute of Teachers of the Disadvantaged in California, Pennsylvania, for six weeks. We decided to take the whole family, which meant our four boys, little Melissa and four foster children. Melissa learned to do without a bottle by throwing it out the window of the van one too many times!

There was no room for us to stay, so they put us up in the Sigma Sigma Sigma sorority house. The boys stayed in their pup tents in the yard many nights.

Since it was, after all, a sorority house, young guys would come around knocking on the door. Melissa was just eighteen-months-old, playing on the porch with the other kids. I remember one young man that saw them, stepped back in the street, look-ing up at the house, confused.

I think we met everyone in that town as we went to the laun-dromat every day.

Manuel enjoyed the institute, working with coal miner chil-dren, some of whom had never been to school.

After that, we took our time, traveling for three months along the East Coast. We learned to avoid the large towns and stopped in the small ones. Manuel and I, with the girls, were in our Starcraft camper and boys in the pup tents. I even cooked in our camper.

When we were in South Carolina, Manuel took the big kids and I to the laundromat, before taking the little ones to play at the park. There were two identical buildings, one which said "white" and the other "colored." Remember, this was the 1960s.

I was confused and, naively, didn't think of racism. "What, I have to wash my whites over there and my darks in the next building?"

Oh, Dorothy," said Manuel. He would say that and roll his eyes whenever I didn't get something.

I went over and talked to a lady on the "colored" side as I was waiting. I told her I had never seen that kind of separation in Kansas. She told me that the Campbell's soup company had a fac-tory there and everyone worked together in the gardens, what-ever their race. But I couldn't wash clothes in the same machine.

We spent a week in Washington D.C. We enjoyed the free museums and national treasures, including the Bureau of Printing and Engraving. At the Smithsonian, I enjoyed seeing Judy Garland's red slippers from the Wizard of Oz. We even met Kansas 5th District Representative Joe Skubitz and took a picture with Melissa on his lap on the steps of the Capitol Building.

WITH REPRESENTATIVE JOE SKUBITZ.

On that trip, "The Sound of Music" film was out in theaters. As a special treat, we decided to take all the kids to see it. When Manuel told them how many tickets we needed, the lady went back to get the manager. We were a little confused.

The manager said, "You have more kids than the VonTrapps! We're going to let you in for free tonight." That was definitely one of our most memorable trips.

What we didn't know, since we didn't have internet or cell phones, was that our daughter Rita had been born in July. We came home to a new baby that August.

Dot's Jots
PUBLISHED AT THE CHRISTMAS SEASON, 1975
Volume 12

Eight girls, two boys, Manuel and Dorothy = 12

I must finish with last year's business before recapping this year. Mainly the end of last year was supposed to have been part of this year's events. Our granddaughter Sara was to have arrived in February. Our son Danny brought Rita C. home at Christmas from Houston to have the baby here. He left Christmas day to return to work. On the 29th of December, we placed a call to him to come back home. He arrived by plane in time for her birth. There was much concern about her, and she did remain in the hospital for ten days. But she is a healthy, lovely baby, and she is our second granddaughter.

The following pictures show how many different modes of transportation we have in this household. We have been impressing on the children about the energy crisis and try to encourage them to ride their bikes as much as possible—have you ever seen so many bicycles? Carol is standing by the new bike rack we purchased this year. The rack has helped in keeping the yard from being cluttered.

The second picture is of Rita on her bike. Martin purchased a three-wheeler this year from paper route money. Ask Martin someday about his first traffic ticket which he received while riding his three-wheeler.

Then Nicky, Melissa and Cindy are enjoying the swings plus the big wooden drum they ride on. The drum turns as they walk on it.

Brian is sitting on the hood of his bright red car. Then come the vehicles we can all go in and do enjoy. Seems we have to have more than the necessary—like a pickup camper plus a crank-up camper—just to get everyone a place to sleep as we travel. We really enjoyed our travels this summer in our pickup camper.

We went north to Minnesota, west to Denver and south to Texas. I said we were going to Houston by way of Minneapolis! That's what we did. We visited family friends in Minnesota—they live on one of those 10,000 lakes. The kids enjoyed boating, fishing, swimming and skiing. Their son, Tim, came back with us. We had all planned to go to Denver, but Manuel's projects piled up.

I have a close school friend who lives in the mountains west of Denver. This trip had been on the agenda, but Manuel said he just didn't have time to go and suggested that the girls and I go ahead. He and the boys stayed behind to work on a house that had lost its roof.

My neighbor, Arlita, decided to go along too, as well as Tim. Christine named this excursion "The Terrible Trip with Ten Women and Tim." The picture of the van with all the girls all over it, plus Tim, is what we rode in to Denver. Tim then caught a direct bus from Denver to Minneapolis.

I will say, after our trips this summer, we did not conform to the energy crisis, and we found traveling to be quite expensive.

Not all of our time is spent in travel. It seems the work goes on and if it weren't for the big kids helping, I'd never make it. Christine and Carolina are shown hanging clothes. Our Maytag washer would make a good advertisement. Not many washing machines have washed clothes for a total of twenty-seven children in twelve years time.

Then there is Joan, who goes off faithfully to Sonic every day and slings "real hamburgers." She has worked there for one and a half years.

We have added and subtracted again this year. For two short weeks, we had an eight-month-old baby and her five-year-old sister. The kids thought it was fun.

We have added in the real estate line also. Ron is shown in front of the purchase this year. He lives in the little house on Dirr Street. In August, just a few days before our trip to Denver, the phone rang, and it was another little girl. Her name is Cindy and she is seven-years-old. She is holding the doll she got on her birthday.

Our last two pictures are our "kids" from Texas. Dan and Rita C. are holding our two grandchildren, Lisa and Sara. Minoru, our "adopted" boy from Japan and his wife, Michiko, are shown standing by Dan and Rita C.'s car. We were so happy they all got to come home for Thanksgiving. Not only were we all together, but their pictures could not have been included in our letter had they not come.

Editorial: This is to let you all know that on December 31st of this year, Manuel and I will have been married for twenty-five years. These have gone by so quickly. They have been years of all kinds of achievements and excitements. He has received a Master's Degree. We've had twenty-seven children in twenty-five years. We have bought (not all paid for yet) six houses. Most of them were junk heaps until Manuel got out his know-how, initiative and hammer, and went to work. We now have two grandchildren and hope to have many more.

God has helped us. He remains an important part of our life. Even though the houses are only material things in our life, it is the children and all the memories they leave for us that we consider the main joy in our life. Our married life is unique. It will never be dull or unmeaningful, because we have so many projects ahead and so many children to share them with. I think it is great.

With these few lines, we wish you the best Christmas yet.

Sincerely, the Manuel Perez family

1970s

Another summer, we traveled to Mexico along with another family and their auntie—a total of seventeen people and two vehicles made up our caravan.

When we arrived in Mexico City, Manuel drove the wrong way at an intersection with large, beautiful fountains. Our friends were behind us and desperate to not lose the only Spanish speaker in the group, they followed right behind Manuel.

We visited many wonderful things and met some of Manuel's long lost cousins.

With seventeen people, we had a lot of dirty clothes and we couldn't find many laundromats. My friend and I saw some women washing their clothes in a stream. We joined them but they had to show us how to beat the clothes on the rocks. I bet that was the first time that a box of Tide had ever been used in that water.

We had tents set up and the boys loved climbing around the mountains. Once, they came back with a rattlesnake, coiled on a stick. Needless to say, Manuel killed their pet pretty quickly!

It was on that trip that we celebrated Rita's fourth birthday with a pinata. Our friends had a little boy too, and we bathed both children in our dishpan.

While in Mexico, we visited an orphanage that our church in Parsons helps to support. We stayed there for a week. I found it an inspiring experience.

As always, we had traveled there in our camper and pup tents. Martin was ten-years-old then and didn't speak Spanish like his father. One day, he came out to the camper with one of the boys, their arms around each other. Martin said, "He wants me to stay all night inside with him."

"How do you know?" I asked. The other boy only spoke Spanish and our boys only spoke a few words of it.

We worked it out with the missionary in charge of the orphanage, who said that was exactly what the boy was asking. So Martin stayed in the orphanage. The next morning, Martin and all the other boys watched from the windows as we fixed our breakfast outside.

We had planned to go to the ancient pyramid miles away from the orphanage. The missionary let two of their young boys, maybe ten or twelve-years-old, go with us as guides. The challenge for the day was for all of us, including me to climb all the way to the top of the pyramid. And so we did. What a day!

When we were ready to leave at around 6 p.m., however, we found that the gates to the park had been closed for the day. We couldn't go back the way we had come, and our young guides didn't know a different way any more than we did. Of course, we didn't have a cell phone—what a dilema.

We wandered around and didn't get back to the orphanage until 1:30 a.m. The missionaries knew we loved kids, and they thought we had departed with two of their boys! They had fixed food for us, on the off chance we were really coming back. We were glad to have found our way.

When we got back to the USA, our friends' auntie was so relieved that she literally kissed the ground!

We went to Mexico a second time, with the younger kids, as our older boys were working at the filing station and on their paper routes.

1990s-2010s

Later, we traveled to Hawaii three times. One summer, we went with my brother, Leonard, and his wife. We rented a car to drive all over the island. When I saw a yard sale sign, I said, "Oh, we have to stop!"

Manuel replied, "How will you be able to bring something home on the plane?" He knew I loved yard sales and stopped anyway. But I did have to wear my purchased blouse home.

On another trip to the islands, our youngest son, Martin, and his wife went with us. We had lots of grandkids at home waiting for souvenirs. There were booths around a large stadium full of wonderful items. My problem was still how to get them home with limited baggage space. The magical red slippers to click three times to go home don't automatically come with the name Dorothy, it seems.

However, I bought fifteen T-shirts anyway. Martin saved the day by offering to put them in his suit bag. Tragically, that bag was lost by the airline. The grandkids were pretty sad to not receive the gifts.

However, we took care of the souvenir problem for our fiftieth wedding anniversary. We took twenty-four family members on a cruise ship for a week. What fun! I can see the kids now. As Manuel and I strolled the ship, we would run into our teenagers, always with a slice of pizza in hand. I think the pizza parlor was open 24/7 and they meant to take advantage of that. The younger grandkids knew where the ice cream machine was, and they gorged on it.

That trip was expensive—to do it, we sold one of our rental houses. And it was well worth it. The kids still talk about it.

Manuel and I also took senior bus trips. Since we had kids in our home for forty-five years, we were the only ones on the bus who had to pay a babysitter. These were usually a one-day trip or an overnighter.

The last long trip Manuel and I took together was to Alaska. We went by bus because we wanted to be able to get off and touch and see. Our voyage was nearly three weeks long total and at the time of year when the Great North has daylight for twenty-four hours a day.

I remember one night as we crawled into bed, Manuel said, "This is the first time I've ever had to wear sunglasses to go to sleep!" I loved that funny man.

On that trip, we went all the way to the North Pole and snapped a picture of me sitting on Santa's lap with the road sign. I also got an Alaska bag.

In 2013, my children got me an eighteen-wheeler truck bed to start filling with my souvenirs and yard sale finds from our years of traveling. But what a load of memories I collected as well.

1960s

As I look back, one of the things I think of is how I was always afraid of leaving a child behind at a gas station while on our long trips. The amazing thing is that didn't happen on a trip, but on a regular Sunday.

We had just gotten home from church and realized three-year-old Melissa was not with us. We hurried back to the church. Everyone was laughing, except Melissa who was crying her heart out.

I guess if one were to lose a child, church would be the best place because God takes care of is all.

CHAPTER SIXTEEN

Feliz Navidad!

HOLIDAY SEASON 1976

Dear Ones,

We shall call this the year of "pain." Usually, I dwell on everything about children but my year started a little differently. You see, I have an annual backache which usually arrives after I start working in the garden in the spring. I have always blamed it on that and after about ten days, it goes away. This year, it started way earlier—wasn't even time for the garden—so into the clinic I go.

My doctor friend takes a picture of my spine. He was concerned with the two lovely kidney stones that also showed up. He packaged up my x-rays and shipped me and them to a urologist in Coffeyville. Immediately, I was told nothing else but surgery. When my friend took me to the hospital the morning of the surgery, and the kids were kissing me goodbye, she said, "I'll bet you are the only one owning jelly-smeared x-rays like other people carry pictures of their kids."

By the time I was wheeled through the swinging doors, my heart was pounding so hard, I feared an attack. I thought someone should know, so I whispered to the guy pushing the cart—I couldn't even talk by this time I was so scared—that my heart was really beating. He sweetly whispered back that he was glad, and within seconds, I knew nothing.

I feel great now, even though I have this embedded stone, which may call for surgery later. The doctor felt it would have damaged my kidney to go after the embedded one.

Guess I really can't refrain from kid talk as that is what goes on here. We have dwindled! Joan was married in August and is living in Minnesota. It is different without her about.

Our count is now only seven and a half, Brian being the half. He is eighteen now and lives across the pasture in one of our houses that Manuel and he are fixing up. Guess you would call him our "backyard kid."

Remember when it was all boys? The six girls are each busy in their own ways. The twins, Christine and Carolina, are on the girls' basketball team. Nicky was active on the girls' soft ball team. Rita and Melissa are both in scouts, doing ceramics and really growing. Cindy just seems to be busy generally.

Even though my count at home is down, I have a new bunch of kids. The principal at Washington School dug me out late in September to become a school lunch aide. In other words, I have a mini-job of two hours a day. Have you ever thought about herding over three hundred kids through their lunches each day and then onto the playground. We really deserve combat pay!

On the playground, you maneuver around past the boys who are shaking down the second graders for their milk money and on beyond to the group destroying themselves on a patch of ice. Then you double back by the kids sailing over the bars on the swing and act like you are going for the group that is putting gravel on the slide, but you don't fiddle with them. You go for the crack-the-whip line.

When the first graders run toward me, I fear they will crash into my incision and I'll have to have emergency help. Like I said, wonder what combat pay amounts to.

I ride my bike to school each day. One of the kids told me the other day that they were going to get me a t-shirt that reads "pedal power." I have pedaled off forty pounds (again) this year. I ride my bike a lot and only hope Santa brings me a big basket for it, then I can even go to the grocery store on it.

Ron is quite busy in his work and this year is making heavy wood furniture, which is interesting and pretty. He does this at home. Did I say my count in kids was down? That is far from true. December 10th, Dan and Rita C., who are still in Houston, presented us with a new grandson. They will be home in a couple days. We can hardly wait to see Jeremiah. Then when you add Joan's husband, Brian, to the list it makes even more. Our list can only get longer and that is the way we like it.

Rita and Melissa are to sing "Silent Night, Holy Night" in Spanish at the church Christmas program on Wednesday. No matter what the language may be, we do wish you a Holy Christmas and want you to know how much each of you means to us.

With all our love,
The Manuel Perez family

IN DOROTHY'S WORDS:

Winner of Parsons Sun's "Most Memorable Christmas Contest" second place prize of $10, 1977

To this household of turmoil and glee a new little face has been added you see...

The story actually started 27 years ago by our marriage as Mexico and Sweden were united. Our marriage has been unique because our family includes the "home grown" type of child and the "gathered in" type.

This brings us to this, our most memorable Christmas. Each year has been a deep memory for us because at each Christmas table we have nearly always had a new face.

But we have two new faces this year. And we still haven't removed the phone, so who knows how many there could be by Christmas?

Our family home now consists of nine children, but we've had at one time or another a total of thirty-two. We'll probably wind up being senior citizens with kids still at home.

Through birth, Mexico and Sweden are represented among the children. Through adoption, Serbia is represented. By opening the door, Japan, Puerto Rico and Hawaii are represented.

And this is our first Christmas to have a black child, which now makes our family complete!

Have you ever thought about having so many kids that you couldn't find enough places to hide presents? So you wrap up the packages and place numbers on them. The kids get disgusted because they don't know which package to shake or squeeze. A master sheet is kept so we remember which number is for which child.

We had a near disaster one year when the master sheet was misplaced!

How neat it is to watch your Japanese boy eat traditional Mexican food with chopsticks!

Children make our Christmas. God's heavenly oven shaded each child a different color, but perfect in His sight.

1920s-1940s
IN MANUEL'S WORDS:

My parents, especially Mom and my sister, Frances, kept an Old Country tradition—the Christmas Posadas. Our house was open to the Mexican community and to the surrounding area for a festive occasion.

This was a welcoming of the Christ Child into our lives, each year renewing our acceptance of Him as the King. The highlight was Mass at midnight at Saint Patrick's. After prayer time, we hosted a social hour with a festive dinner—lots of good Mexican food to eat for everyone. It was a special meal as we fasted during the day prior to taking communion. One must remember that the Catholic family's dedication to Catholicism is deeply rooted in faith to the Divine Being.

It was a time of revelry and sharing, the true love of kinship and friends who respectfully were obedient to this time of year. So much was given and so many that cared. There was a personal touch that was meaningful to each.

My sister, Frances, set the house in order to receive our guests. She decorated whole rooms as a manger scene with mountains made from paper bags and painted trees. Joe was instrumental in building the framework of the manger. Dad and other family members and friends helped with preparing the nativity too. For the children, there was a pinata.

Traditionally, the celebration continues until January when the wise men arrive to visit the Christ child. At that time, adults celebrated their gift of love of family.

For me, it was a classic season for being a kid and doing what kids do. The weather seemed right. We went sledding, snow-balling and generally playing in the snow.

Now it's a time of reflecting on the emotional spirit of the past that comes alive in very real forms. We experience the personal touch of love, in reverence for our Diety and for one another. For those of us that still remain Catholic, the Mass is reminiscent of the spirit of the past.

Christmas 1981

Even though the time is here,
I'd better get started earlier this year
    You see, I really missed sending my letter the last season
    So, if I get on with it now, there will be no excuse or reason
        The thing we wanted to tell you about last year, which we think is so cool
        Yes, we built us a great big in-ground pool
        Now all summer long we swim and we dive
        The kids bring more friends and our home has more jive.
            The year of this wedding—Ron and Sonia
            The year of the kitchen—I've got a new big one.
            And to top off this year—I've just been employed by the Tri-County Special Ed Cooperative (this is the Coop employing Manuel) to be an aide to a blind boy at the Parsons Junior High School. I am his constant partner and after just a few days, I've learned that I am the one

doing the learning. He reads to me from his Braille books. I give his math problems to him and he does them with his Chinese abacus. I even have to go to the boys' gym classes with him, but the coach actually does exercises with him.

You know we built the pool a year ago this summer. One project creates another one. Just had to have the kitchen off the pool. This is the third kitchen in our home. Poor Manuel has plumbing all under the house. If it ever leaks, we could possibly have a fountain or shower in any of the rooms (haha). Besides, my other kitchen was so small and now we have our big table and chairs in this kitchen. We move kitchens like other people move furniture. I am just as thrilled about what is happening to the old one—even though it was small for a kitchen, it is super for a sewing room.

Have you ever been called collect from Disneyland? Melissa took her first trip by air. She went to California to visit my brother, Leonard, and his family. Their daughter Debbie is Melissa's age. Of course, this trip was not without events—the airline strike happened and she was without a flight in Denver. Thanks to my friend, Ruth, who lives there, she got onto a later flight.

We did not travel this summer. We are content to be here with the pool. We keep our Starcraft camper up all summer and when the nights are really hot, we sleep in it. One morning, Manuel said, "It is just like being in a KOA Campground. We get up out of the camper and go jump in the pool." We love it.

CHAPTER SEVENTEEN

Growing Old Together

IN DOROTHY'S WORDS:

For our twenty-fifth wedding anniversary in 1975, Manuel gave me a beautiful eternity ring with eighteen diamonds.

I love my jewelry, however by 2007, I couldn't wear my wedding ring on my left hand. I had a mastectomy surgery where twenty-two lymph nodes were removed—now, my left arm and hand are constantly swelling.

In the months before our anniversary in December, I came up with an idea involving that ring. When I asked him, Manuel thought it would be wonderful. I designed necklaces and wrote identical letters to my girls, with a personal word to each.

December 2007
"From Here to Eternity"

Dear Selena,

This letter was inspired from the quote above. It was our twenty-fifth wedding anniversary that Grandpa gave me an eternity ring. How beautiful and thoughtful.

Family is the most important treasure that we have. Of course, God is the One who helped us create our family and I thank Him every day for that.

I had been thinking of how I would pass my idea on to eternity. Not that I didn't love my ring—I just wanted to share! Well the light bulb turned on in my head. There were eighteen diamonds in my ring. We have two daughters and seven granddaughters. Meaning two diamonds a piece and we've added your birth stones to the diamonds.

We dreamed up the design and the jewelers made them from the ring. Everyone at the jewelry store thought it was so special and we hope you will enjoy your necklace. Maybe you could pass it on down someday to someone special. Then you could add another birth stone.

We love you so much and remember "when prayers go up, blessings come down."

Love, Grandma and Grandpa

P.S. I will always treasure the trips you came to see me. You came by walking, on your bike, on your scooter, on your motorcycle...and then we made cookies! Love ya.

Our granddaughter, Selena, was little when I gave the necklace to her. Her mother, Sonia, kept it for her. The fall of 2013, Sonia brought it out and gave Selena the letter. Sonia said there were a few tears. Selena wore her necklace for the first time at the junior/senior prom.

1980s

IN DOROTHY'S WORDS:

We had gone to a reunion with Melissa's "roots," as we called her biological family. On the way home, we stopped to visit our friends, the Urbans, in Wichita. Manuel went to see a camper he had been interested in. We ended up buying it—a HiLo. With the punch of a button, we had an instant camper. I thought of all the times we set up tents and cranked up our StarCraft camper. We made a lot of memories, though.

We assumed we'd be taking many long trips since Manuel had retired from the public school in 1986. However, back and hip x-rays resulted in long surgeries.

The new camper served another purpose as a hospital recovery room because it had air conditioning. We parked it by the pool that July so Manuel could recuperate and watch us. When company came, they had a nice place to stay too.

While Manuel was recuperating, he got a call from our community college. They said they could certainly use his abilities, so instead of retiring, he taught at the learning center, helping people to get G.E.D.s and assisting the foreign students with their English. He enjoyed only worked twenty hours a week.

1990s
IN MANUEL'S WORDS:
The big "70" is only days away. No, it's not a symbol of my end—

however, it does awaken me to another phase of life. I feel I'd like to celebrate the adventure by doing a bit of traveling. No longer the 8 a.m.- 5 p.m. call of a routine. A feeling of less anxiety and stress, with time not being dictated by the calendar day nor the hour hand.

Couple to Celebrate 50 Years:
Parsons Sun, December 2000

Mr. and Mrs. Manuel Perez, 1118 Dorothy, will celebrate

MANUEL AND DOROTHY

142

their 50th wedding anniversary with a reception hosted by their family beginning at 1 p.m. Sunday, January 14, at the First Foursquare Church in Parsons.

The couple had taken a cruise with 24 of their family members Dec. 18-23, touring Cozumel and Cancun, Mexico.

Manuel C. Perez and Dorothy L. Meier were married Dec. 31, 1950, in Huntsville, Ark.

Mr. Perez is retired. He taught for the Tri-County Special Education Cooperative in Parsons schools for 37 years. Mrs. Perez has been a cashier for Wal-Mart for 18 years and formerly worked at the First National Bank for 25 years as a teller.

Mr. Perez serves on the Parsons Board of Zoning Adjustments and is a former board member for the Kansas Children's Service League in Wichita. He also served on both the advisory boards for Belmont Towers and the Labette Correctional Conservation Camp.

The couple are members of the First Foursquare Church. They have lived in Parsons since their marriage.

The couple have eight children, Daniel Perez of Wichita, Ron Perez, Brian Perez, Martin Perez, Melissa Perez-Lambkins, Rita Perez, Ronald Perez and Fredline Kelsey, all of Parsons. They have 14 grandchildren, and five great-grandchildren. They have been foster parents to many children over the years. Friends and family are invited to attend the reception. The couple request no gifts.

Thank You note from Manuel:

How inspiring and wonderful that you helped us remember that first step in our maturing years!

It's this 50th that has caused us, with your cards and letters, to reflect upon the events of previous years, the expression of Our Living Faith.

Not only your thoughts and expressions of endearment, but the reception presented by our children and loved ones: WOW!

As we celebrate this occasion, it becomes easy to recognize the precious gifts of life that God has given us. As I said in my opening sentence, when we were married we didn't know the precious gift of people who helped us identify our spiritual gifts.

The gift of our children, the opportunity to us, our gift of compassion (foster children). He has given us opportunities to use His spiritual gift in many ways. He has given us the gift of many dear friends.

Thank you for your presence and rememberances. Thank you, dear family, for the wonderful reception. We couldn't have had this moment of joy without you.

Thanks,

Dad

IN MANUEL'S WORDS:

Many times in my adult life Mom's vision has appeared, a dream or beautiful remembrance that comes back in this form. Dad, Joe, Mom. Short and fleeting, yet with a hidden message, probably something I'd been thinking about.

Dad came to me recently when I was making a decision. His message was "don't be hateful." Perhaps during a time when I was disappointed.

2000s

IN DOROTHY'S WORDS:

I retired from Wal-mart at age seventy-eight, after twenty-three years of service. On the news, I saw a ninety-one-year-old woman working at a convenience store when it was robbed—she beat the socks off the robber! I loved my job and my customers—if she was working at ninety-one, then maybe I could go back now at age eighty-two.

A friend helped me make a quilt with a cheery red background, with pieces of my Wal-Mart vests. The other side has red stars and my children's names, biological and adopted. One star has our wedding date. They are connected with dozens of scraps from clothes I made for the kids over the years.

DOROTHY AND HER QUILT.

At eighty-six-years-old, I call these my "golden years." A glance at my calendar for January shows appointments with a foot doctor, an ear/nose/throat doctor, an eye doctor, a heart doctor, a cancer doctor and then my own doctor. That's where all my gold goes.

People have said they can't wait to be a senior, that it looks like such fun to go on trips and such. But they don't know all the aches and pains, what with my insulin for diabetes and oral chemotherapy for leukemia.

A few years ago, I had a very hoarse voice that wouldn't go away. The doctor found a nodule on my vocal chords. He removed it in a simple surgery. "That's the same surgery that Julie Andrews had," he mentioned. "Hers was caused by all her singing. I wonder what caused yours."

"I guess it was from hollering at too many kids," I replied.

When I was a little girl, Mom and Dad said I did backbends and flipflops, standing on my head. Every time my grandma saw me, she would say, "Dotty, I never know who you are until when you are standing on your feet."

In high school, I led the band in the parade through Liberty. I was the acrobatic baton twirler. You should see me now. I depend on my cane to walk and I doubt I could even stand up to twirl it.

In the doctor's office, they ask, "How are you doing, Dorothy?"

"I'm fine," I say. And by the grace of God, I am, because I have a wonderful family and our marriage was super and different.

CHAPTER EIGHTEEN

Saying Goodbye

Late 1990s

IN DOROTHY'S WORDS:

My mom lived with us for her last year and a half of life. I treasured that time with her.

She had been living on her own but was getting a little lost. She kept unplugging the refrigerator to "save electricity" so my sister-in-law Norma and I would take turns taking meals to her.

My brother, Leonard, who was a career Navy man, was coming to town to visit. Mom called him her "distant relative" because we didn't seem him much. I brought Mom to our house for a good bath before my brother's arrival.

DOROTHY'S PARENTS, MILBERT AND GEORGIA MEIER.

We were sitting on the couch talking and Mom said, "Well, now how long have I lived here, Dorothy?"

I didn't know what to say, but I was pleased for the opportunity. "You've been here quite a while now, Mom. And it's so nice having you." She never asked to go back home. It was such an easy transition.

I still worked part-time at Wal-mart, so Manuel would stay with her. One day at lunch, Mom had cleaned her plate. She looked at Manuel and asked innocently, "Do I need to eat the flowers on the plate too?"

We put her in the bedroom next to the bathroom. Mom knew her way to the kitchen after that, but if she turned to the front room, she'd be lost.

Mom had two pairs of shoes. When Manuel couldn't find his shoes, she'd have lined his up with hers under her bed. She would find his glasses and then wear them on top of her head.

When she got colon cancer, we had hospice help come in—I think that's one reason that our daughter Melissa went into social work.

We set up chairs in Mom's bedroom, so the grandkids could just come and sit with her. Leonard spent the last six weeks here with her.

Mom played the piano by ear. At Christmas, we brought a keyboard into her room and laid it across her knees. We all assembled and requested songs. She'd play, running her hands up and down that keyboard.

She knew every word of the Bible. I have her Swedish Bible, even though I can't read it.

Mom was bedridden, but the January day she died, she just sat up suddenly, with the most wonderful expression on her face. We knew she saw Heaven that day.

IN MANUEL'S WORDS:

Mom and Dad attended my KSTC graduation. I later overheard Dad tell our relative who was visiting from Trinidad, Colorado, that I was a professor. It left me with the impression that Dad was justly proud.

It made me proud that in his later years, Dad allowed me to care for him. I can't forget Dad's non-verbal way of beckoning me to look after Mom, as he lay slowly, but silently slipping away. My brother Joe left me to take care of the love Dad left behind. I wasn't present when Dad went away, but he has always been near—his love for the welfare of his family will always be remembered. I'm sure Dad knew when I came to visit his mortal resting place. Mom and Dad left me a wealth of solace.

My older brother Joe was, and in memory is still, an inspiration. So often as I remodel a house, I reflect on his teaching.

Something that often comes to mind is my free use of his Indian head pennies that he used to keep in a baking powder canister. How he allowed me to change candy at Ed Spooner's candy shop. I never can come up with a time, if ever, that he scolded me. But I know that I must have abused the privilege.

Perhaps I paid part of it back as I mixed plaster mud for him. Gosh, I worked my butt off trying to keep up with him splashing plaster. He was a comfort on a worksite. I never had any doubts about how to go about a task. Somehow the job always got done but I felt his reassurance as I worked along.

I remember his kindness to Mom and Dad. I was there when he arrived home from service in WWII—what a blessing for my parents to receive their son safe! After Dad's retirement, Joe cared for him. In Mother's presence, Joe asked me if I would care for her should he ever be absent.

Dad, my inspiration. Mom, my motivation. Joe, Frances, Mike, my mentors.

PHOTO CREDIT PARSONS SUN.

Maria Perez Celebrates 100th Year
by Connie Brown of the Sun Staff, January 1986

Maria G. Perez, 822 N. Central observed her 100th birthday on January 12.

Still living in her own home, she uses a walker to get around inside. Until the past few years, Mrs. Perez enjoyed doing hand work of all kinds, especially crocheting and embroidery. She has also enjoyed raising flowers and house plants, and her pets. She currently has two cats.

A daughter, Delores (Lola) Braden, and son-in-law live with Mrs. Perez and care for her. Two other children, Manuel and Mike, also live in Parsons. Three children are deceased, and she has 10 grandchildren and numerous great-grandchildren.

Mrs. Perez is a native of Mexico. She speaks little English although while her health permitted her to be active, she knew enough to manage grocery shopping and calling a taxi, Manuel said.

She was born January 12, 1886, at Penjamo, Mexico. She came to Parsons with her husband, Jose Perez, in 1916. He worked as a section crew for the Katy Railroad.

They celebrated their 50th wedding anniversary on February 24, 1958. He died August 5, 1966.

Manuel said his mother really enjoyed the Christmas Posadas, a re-enactment of Mary and Joesph's journey to Bethlehem and the difficulties they encountered.

Through the years, Mrs. Perez kept the tradition for the Hispanic community, and Manuel said many in the community still remember the wonderful food she served.

2009
IN DOROTHY'S WORDS:

In August, a wind storm had blown branches down on the garage, and Manuel had been clearing them off. It was a Friday, and I was going to go to the grocery store. "Do you want to come with me?" I asked.

"No, I better go over and finish those limbs," Manuel said.

When I got back, Rita was on the phone calling 911. He was on the floor, still alive. The ambulance took him to the hospital.

The doctor examined him and then told me, "His heart is just as strong as can be."

"Oh, good," I thought, relieved. "He's going to make it!"

Then the doctor said the words that changed my world. "But he'll never come to.".

Manuel had had a blood clot in his brain that had burst. They couldn't even operate—it wouldn't have done any good. There was nothing more they could do but put Manuel on life support.

We had both signed "do not resuscitate" orders. So the next day, Saturday, we took him off the life support and brought him home. I had always thought that folks died instantly when the support was taken away, but he was breathing well. Manuel lived until Monday morning.

We had his bed in the front room, and people would come and sit with him. At 4 a.m. the door bell rang. It was our daughter Melissa's recently divorced husband, Greg. "I just have to see Grandpa one last time," he said in tears.

Manuel passed away at 8:15 a.m. Monday, August 24, 2009, at the age of eighty-six.

IN MARTIN'S WORDS:

Dad, you have been the father to many children and adults. It made me jealous as a child to share you when I was growing up. As an adult, I know it was God who put you in that place—for all the people who needed a father. I realized that as I got older. Thank you for being my father on Earth.

IN MARTIN'S DAUGHTER, RACHELLE'S, WORDS:

During the past few years, I've spent time with Grandma and Lisa helping in the sewing room. We even finished a quilt together. We had planned a trip to Joplin to get supplies and materials from JoAnn's. Grandpa started out on our trip and I buckled up in the backseat. If you were a grandkid, you would know why we all buckled up when Grandpa would drive.

We got halfway to Joplin before I piped up. "Grandpa, can I drive?" I started listing off how qualified I was for the job and asked again.

Grandpa laughed and said, "No, no, you drive too slow."

"No, I drive five miles over the speed limit."

He said, "I know."

I looked up at the speedometer and Grandpa was driving 80 mph in a 55 mph zone. I never asked again.

IN MELISSA'S DAUGHTER, JADE'S, WORDS:

"If you need anything, just ask. I'm always here," Grandpa would tell me constantly. I know he's still there and all that I need to do is ask.

The many attempts to go to Grandma's and Grandpa's house to clean were well worth it. The attempts to throw away Grandma's outdated food had to be the hardest ones. Grandpa was always in the back saying, "Oh, Dorothy!" Then he would give me the chance to throw away the food.

Then there were Grandpa's many history lessons. I still have the amazing stamp collection that Grandpa gave me. He told me about each stamp and the significance of each one. I'll always keep and cherish it and hopefully add a couple unique stamps to it myself.

DOROTHY SURROUNDED BY FAMILY AT MANUEL'S
FUNERAL, INCLUDING MINORU AND CHRISTINE.

Parsons Sun
August 29-30, 2009

Manuel Perez, who died Monday at his home, dedicated his life to his family and to improving the lives of children.

And that's probably an understatement for all that he's accomplished in this community. He was, after all, a husband, a father, a foster parent, a long-time teacher and a tireless worker.

Many methods can be used to measure a man, but we all could strive to learn from Mr. Perez' life by being more involved with our families and our communities. He had earned associate's, bachelor's and master's degrees, working his way through school. His longest teaching stint after graduation was in Parsons schools, where he taught special education from 1963 to 1986. He later worked at Labette Community College.

Over the years, the Sun has done several stories on Mr. Perez and his accomplishments and his family. Most recently we wrote about his induction into the Kansas Children's Service League Hall of Fame for his 45 years of service to Kansas children.

Mr. Perez leaves behind a wife and a large family, with their own memories of their husband, father, grandfather, great-grandfather. His community should remember him as well.

A letter from Manuel's coworker

Dear Dorothy and Family,

After attending the funeral on Thursday, I knew that I had to write you and tell you how I felt about this man you called "father," "grandfather" and "husband."

First of all, let me say that Manuel Perez was my friend and had been for over thirty years. We were not the kind of friends that watched sporting events, phoned daily or emailed each other. In fact, it was a fairly rare event when we got to see each other (most recently). On the occasion that we did bump into each other, it was as if we had been together the evening before and were merely finishing up on a conversation we had just had.

Not only did I respect and admire Manuel, I liked what I saw and heard. We were pretty much eye-to-eye on many things, in thought as well as height. I saw Manuel Perez as a direct talking, honest, hard-working man who loved people. You could tell that he led a disciplined life and brooked no laziness in

155

himself or anybody who hung around him. His sense of humor transcended all of that and no conversation between us was without it.

In one half-hour visit, I could learn thirty little tidbits on "how to," "the why's" or "the if's" and how they played out in the grand scheme of things, each replete with its own little saying. I cherish those spare moments we shared and will always, always be grateful that God let me get to know Manuel Perez.

I could spend fifty paragraphs trying to explain what Manuel meant to me but I know you understand when I say it still would not capture my thoughts. Instead, let me finish by saying, to me, Manuel Perez was like that special spice a cook stirs into their favorite recipe. Without that spice, the food is not quite as tasty. Manuel was that spice and my life will be less for my loss.

To you, Dorothy, I offer my affection and regards. Thanks to you and Manuel for allowing me to be part of your family. My wife and I will remember you all in our prayers.

God bless,

Jody and Joan Thompson

FROM MANUEL:
"I'll be seeing you"

Music awakens from within a very compelling sense of humility. This to me is a summons for prayer. Music met with my faith. For I've not seen my God. But what's to keep me from thinking about Him in my moments of leisure. I believe God exists.

Music has become a way of life for me. To preface this, I'll say I yearned for a way to pray in a meaningful way in my daily ventures of life.

I wish you a safe and inspirational journey. Do you remember the song "Always?"

Always by Irving Berlin
Everything went wrong
And the whole day long
I'd feel so blue
For the longest while
I'd forget to smile then I met you
Now that my blue days have passed
Now that I've found you at last
I'll be loving you always
With a love that's true always
When the things you've planned
Need a helping hand
I will understand always
Always
Days may not be fair always
That's when I'll be there always
Not for just an hour
Not for just a day
Not for just a year
But always

To Daniel, Ron, Brian, Martin, Mel and Rita, and to all that meet each new day with thoughts of the beauty of His creation. Fantastic. You've been given one more day. Should you hear a song upon the wonder of God's nature that recalls a memory we shared...Please do not let the thought of me cause sadness. Rather be joyous that we shared these few precious moments together.

CHAPTER NINETEEN

What I'm Going to Be

IN DOROTHY'S WORDS:
What am I going to be when they grow up? I have asked myself that question over the years. I guess I am what I always was—happy to be part of over ninety children's lives.

I want to express that each child who has touched our hearts is so very important to us. Thank you, each and everyone. You made our life very special.

Even though I have so many more stories to talk about, I'll finish this book with a letter that a dear friend and Wal-Mart coworker, Eudora Evans, gave me on my seventy-fifth birthday. She calls me "Oh, Dorothy" as Manuel did.

2003 "Oh Dorothy"

They say, "it takes a village to raise a child." For Dorothy Perez—it took Dorothy to raise a village.

Dorothy was a mother to ninety-four children and her own, her grandchildren and great-grandchildren. Not to leave out the love of her life, Manuel.

So many people know Dorothy better than I (I've only known her less than a year) with her caring heart, love for life, her overwhelming sense of humor, her statured character. She is a solid naturer of all, always giving so much of herself to her family and friends.

My life would not be complete had I not met Dorothy and heard her stories, from the two laundry houses, the piano in the bathroom, the awesome swimming pool in the backyard to the wonderful "Flake bread."

Dorothy's faith in her God...if we could only have a pinch as much faith in God as she. Dorothy is now going through some medical difficulties yet knows her faith will pull her through. As she said to her doctor, "Oh, it's just another experience. Wonder what's next."

Dorothy is happy in the kitchen with her children and grandchildren, making a huge batch of enchiladas, Flake bread or at the swimming pool with her family and friends.

Her home started out as a four room house and has now expanded to a wonderful hacienda. There is a yellow brick road in the back with all her children's names and birthdays.

Dorothy is so proud of her childrens' and friends' accomplishments. She never leaves one out, making everyone so loved by "oh, Dorothy."

Dorothy it is by chance we could be sisters, but it is with our hearts we are friends—may our stories never end. Love you, Dorothy.

Eudora Evans

Acknowledgements

THANK YOU TO DOROTHY PEREZ and her family for opening their stories to me.

Thank you to my parents and mentors, Don and Michelle Ruebke. Thank you to Larry and Taunya Rutenbeck for their encouragement and support. I'd like to thank my other half—my husband, Vincent. Also my wonderful copyeditors, Ashley Bergner and Jan Bloom. Thanks to Adrian Buentello for his cheerful cover artwork. Thanks to the CreateSpace team for their help and expertise.

I'd also like to acknowledge my Grandma Lida Overton, who brought this story to my attention. She has been Dorothy's friend for many years and taught at the same Tri-County Co-Op as Manuel.

I'm honored to have been a part of this work.
- Jenna Quentin